Jane Bull

Knit It, Stitch It!

Knit It, Stitch It!

Jane Bull

DK

LONDON, NEW YORK, MUNICH,
MELBOURNE, AND DELHI

For Stephen,
Charlotte, Billy,
and James

DESIGN • Jane Bull
SENIOR EDITOR • Ros Walford
DTP DESIGNER • David McDonald
ASSOCIATE PUBLISHER • Nigel Duffield

First published in Great Britain in 2010 by
Dorling Kindersley Limited
80 Strand, London WC2R 0RL
A Penguin Company

This edition produced for The Book People,
Hall Wood Avenue, Haydock,
St. Helens WA11 9UL

Contains content from:
Change Your Room, The Christmas Book,
The Crafty Art Book, The Holiday Activity Book,
Made by Me, Made by Me Too, Make it
The Merry Christmas Activity Book,
The Rainy Day Book,
The Sunny Day Book.

A CIP catalogue record for this book
is available from the British Library

ISBN: 978-1-4053–6173-6

Printed and bound by
L Rex Printing Co, China.

discover more at
www.dk.com

Knit It, Stitch It!

Knitting 8

Knitting 10
Knitting dolls 12
Handy knits 14
Lots of loops 16
Knitting with needles 18
How to knit "knit stitch" 20
Knit a blanket 24
Knitted purses 26
Krazy knits 28
Knitted pals 30
Making Ted 32
Ted's friends 34
Woolly hats 36
Big knitting! 38

Fun with Wool 40

Woolly webs 42
Get weaving 46
Keep on weaving 48

Stitches and embroidery 50

Made by me workboxes 52
Embroidery 54
Stitch directory 56
Decorate a T-shirt 57
Picture stitches 58
T-shirt 60
Cross-stitch 62
Pixel pix 68

Sewing projects 70

Sewing 72
Pouches 74
Pirate Pete 76
Meet the gang 78
Throw together Pete 80
Pocket lockets 82
Hanging softies 84
Felt flowers 86
Bags of ribbons 88
Customize cushions 90
Scrap bags 94
Throw together a scrap bag 96
Hello Dolly! 98
Goodnight Dolly! 99

Make your own
two-sided doll 100
Sew Dolly's faces 102
Make Dolly's clothes 103
Dolly pattern 104
Lavender bags 106
Patchwork patterns 108
Packing presents 110
Winter woollies 112
How to stitch some woollies 114
Button badges 116
Cup cakes 118
Fold-away game mats 120
Cover up! 122
Transform your clothes 124
Fabric 126
Rag mats 128
Making friends 130
Hold onto your hats! 132
How to make Bob Bobble 133
Pocket purses 134
How to make a glam bag 136
Comfy cushions 138
Crafty kit 140

Templates 142
Index 143–44

Knitting

Knitting

Learn to knit and you will be able to make anything from hats and scarves to bracelets and purses.

Knitting doll

Knitting dolls are a great way to knit long cords of wool.

10 mm needles

Different colour needles help you work out which way to start knitting again when you stop half way through a row.

4 mm needles

Knitting yarn

This comes in various thicknesses and can be made from wool, nylon, or cotton. The projects in this book are mainly made from wool called double knit (DK) – not too thick and not too thin.

Needles

There are several sizes of knitting needle. The mm size refers to the thickness of the needle. When you are learning to knit, it helps to use short needles as they are easiest to handle.

Embroidery needles

Large needles, with blunt ends and big eyes, are best for sewing together wool at the end of a project.

Scissors

Knitted cords

Stitches

Rows

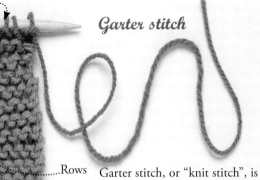

Garter stitch

Garter stitch, or "knit stitch", is the most simple kind to learn.

Knitting

What is knitting? Knitting uses needles to work yarn into interlocking loops (stitches) to form a fabric. There are lots of stitches you can use to make fabric look different.

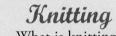
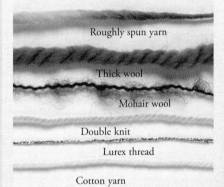

Roughly spun yarn

Thick wool

Mohair wool

Double knit

Lurex thread

Cotton yarn

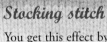

Stocking stitch

You get this effect by knitting rows in purl stitch, then knit stitch. In this book you will learn how to do knit stitch.

You can buy a knitting doll or make your own.

Which wool?
Any wool will work, but try using up leftover yarn – it's great for making long, stripy cord.

The stitches are made at the top of the doll.

Knitting dolls

These are a super-simple way to make colourful cord. Turn the cord into bracelets or use it on projects in this book.

Knitting pin or embroidery needle with a blunt end

The knitted cord comes out of the bottom of the doll.

The cord is a knitted tube.

Dollies
Knitting dolls are available from toy shops and craft shops.

Make your own doll

Slip the paper clips, evenly spaced, onto the empty reel. Wrap lots of sticky tape around them to hold them firmly in place.

You will need:

empty sticky tape reel

4 paper clips

embroidery needle

sticky tape

Cast on

1. Take a ball of yarn and thread the end through the top of the spool.

2. Wrap the yarn around the first clip.

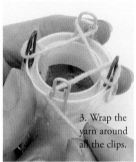

3. Wrap the yarn around all the clips.

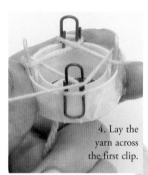

4. Lay the yarn across the first clip.

Making stitches...

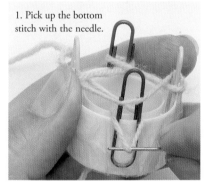

1. Pick up the bottom stitch with the needle.

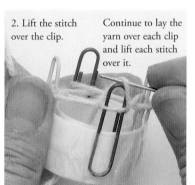

2. Lift the stitch over the clip. Continue to lay the yarn over each clip and lift each stitch over it.

The cord starts to appear...

... Casting off

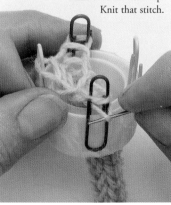

1. Lift the last stitch you made onto the next clip. Knit that stitch.

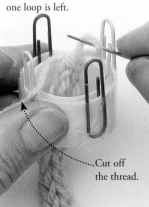

Repeat step 1 until just one loop is left.

...Cut off the thread.

To finish, pass the thread through the last loop and pull it tight.

Handy tip

This homemade doll makes a thicker cord than the shop-bought one.

Handy knits

Can't find any knitting needles?

Then use your fingers instead. It's the handiest way to make brightly coloured belts and friendship bracelets.

You will need:
- yarns – thick or thin
- your fingers

Cast on

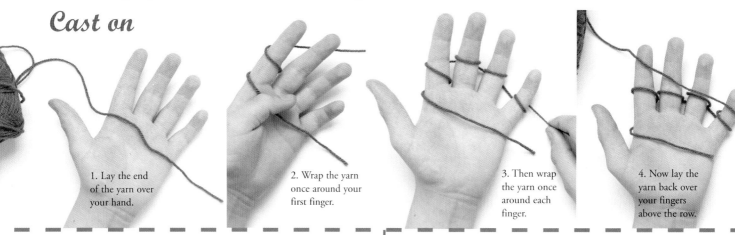

1. Lay the end of the yarn over your hand.

2. Wrap the yarn once around your first finger.

3. Then wrap the yarn once around each finger.

4. Now lay the yarn back over your fingers above the row.

Knit a row...

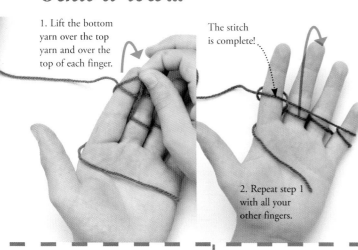

1. Lift the bottom yarn over the top yarn and over the top of each finger.

The stitch is complete!

2. Repeat step 1 with all your other fingers.

... and the next rows

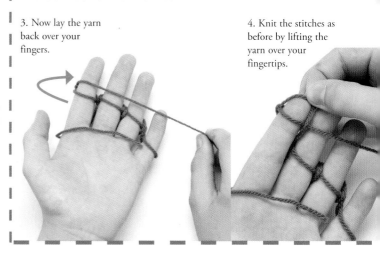

3. Now lay the yarn back over your fingers.

4. Knit the stitches as before by lifting the yarn over your fingertips.

Pull into shape

Turn your hand over.

Pull the end of the yarn and the knitting should make a sausage shape.

Finish off

1. Lift the first stitch off your finger.

2. Put it on the next finger.

3. Knit the stitch as above by lifting one over the other.

4. Repeat this until you have one stitch left.

Cut off yarn here.

Lift the last stitch off your finger.

Thread the end of the yarn through the loop and pull tight.

Handy tip
Don't pull the yarn too tight or it will be difficult to move the stitches on your fingers.

Mix them up
When you've got the hang of hand knitting, try mixing your colours by knitting with two or three yarns at once.

Lots of loops

Make colourful braids

by simply tying slipknots one after the other. Use as bracelets, or accessories for your clothes.

Loop lots of colourful yarns at the same time.

Make a loop...

Long end

1. Wrap the end of the yarn around two fingers.

2. Make a loop in the long end of the yarn. Poke it up between your fingers.

3. Pull the loop through.

4. Pull the yarn tight to secure the loop.

... make another loop...

5. Open up the loop.

6. Pinch another loop in the long end of the yarn. Pull it through the first loop.

7. Pull the yarn tight so the second loop sits on top of the first.

Scraps of yarn

Double yarn braid

Tie ends into a bow.

Tiny single yarn braid

Your braids make ideal friendship bracelets. Or tie them to bags or use as hair bands.

Lurex thread

... keep making loops...

Repeat steps
5, 6, and 7.

Continue until the braid is long
enough...

...to fit round your wrist.

How to stop

1. Snip off the yarn.

2. Push the end of the yarn
through the last loop...

...and pull tight.

Mix and match
Try bunching lots of
wool together and braiding
as one piece. Use chunky
yarn for thicker braids and
shiny lurex for sparkle!

Knitting with needles

Needle

....Loops called
stitches

Rows

Ball of yarn

Here is a piece of knitting - it has been made using a simple knitting stitch called "knit stitch". When lots of rows of knit stitch are knitted together they are known as "garter stitch".

Keep knitting and this piece
....will grow longer and longer.

Slip-knot

The first stitch on the needle is knotted so the yarn stays on.

Pull the ends of the yarn tight –
now you have the first stitch.

Take a ball of yarn and make a loop at the end.

Bring the yarn through the loop to create a new loop.

Keep pulling the new loop through.

Attach the new loop to the needle.

Casting on
There are many ways to cast on. This method uses the thumb.

Wrap the yarn around your thumb as shown.

....Pick up the yarn with the needle.

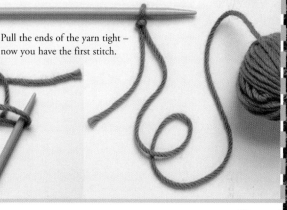

Let the yarn go from your thumb onto the needle.

Continue doing this...

... until you have enough stitches.

How many?

The projects in this book tell you how many stitches to cast on. Lots of stitches give you a wide fabric, while few stitches make a narrow fabric.

Now you are ready to KNIT!

Stitches 1 2 3 4 5...

When you are......
starting a new row, start with the first stitch on the right and work towards the left.

The yarn will be on the right as well.

How to knit "knit stitch"

Two ways to knit - the steps below show two different ways to do knit stitch. Have a go and see which method suits you best. Left-handers often find the second method easiest.

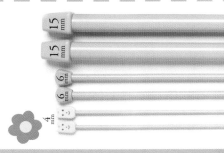

1 Try this way...
There's a rhyme by the numbers below. Learn it – it might help you remember how to knit!

Stitches cast on ready for knitting

Try putting the yarn between the fingers on your right hand so you don't have to move your whole hand to make a stitch.

1 Under the fence
Hold the needle with the stitches on it in your left hand.

Push the right-hand needle through the first stitch.

2 Catch the sheep
Take the yarn behind the needles...

... and bring it back to the front between the needles.

Casting off - how to stop
Take away the stitches one by one.

1. Knit two stitches.

2. Lift the second stitch over the first stitch...

... and over the tip of the needle.

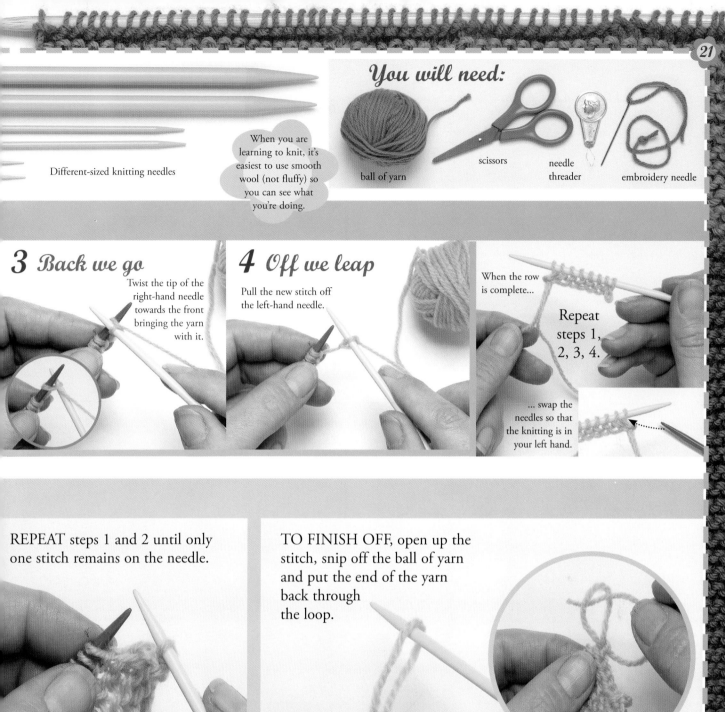

Different-sized knitting needles

When you are learning to knit, it's easiest to use smooth wool (not fluffy) so you can see what you're doing.

You will need:

ball of yarn

scissors

needle threader

embroidery needle

3 Back we go

Twist the tip of the right-hand needle towards the front bringing the yarn with it.

4 Off we leap

Pull the new stitch off the left-hand needle.

When the row is complete...

Repeat steps 1, 2, 3, 4.

... swap the needles so that the knitting is in your left hand.

REPEAT steps 1 and 2 until only one stitch remains on the needle.

TO FINISH OFF, open up the stitch, snip off the ball of yarn and put the end of the yarn back through the loop.

Pull the thread tight.

2 ... or this way

Try this if you are left-handed.

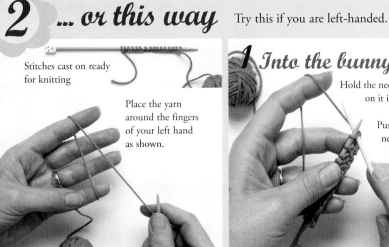

Stitches cast on ready
for knitting

Place the yarn
around the fingers
of your left hand
as shown.

1 Into the bunnyhole

Hold the needle with stitches
on it in your left hand.

Push the right-hand
needle through the
first stitch.

2 Run around the tree

Wrap the yarn around
the needle and pull it
down between
the needles.

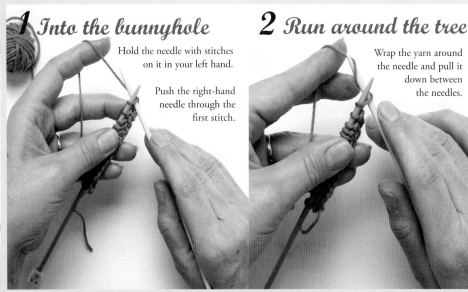

Sew in your ends

Thread each end onto
an embroidery needle.

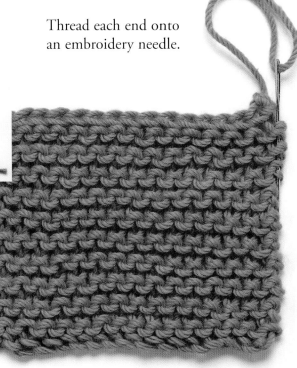

Push the needle
down through
the edge of the
knitting –
about the first
five rows.

When the piece of
knitting is complete,
neaten it up by
sewing in the ends.

Snip off
the yarn.

3 *Out of the bunnyhole* 4 *Away runs he*

Bring the right-hand needle to the front bringing the yarn with it.

Pull the new stitch off the left-hand needle.

When the row is complete...

... turn the needle over and hold it in your left hand.

Repeat steps 1, 2, 3, 4.

Sew up seams

Place two pieces of knitting together.

Knot the yarn and sew it so it goes inside the seam.

Sew over the edge of the knitting – then fasten off by sewing down the edge.

Cut off thread.

24

Knit a blanket

Once you have got the hang of finger knitting, you will have a good idea how to cast on to needles and start knitting. Using plain stitch you can make a finger puppet from a single square, and if you get really ambitious you can make lots of squares to make a blanket.

I'm in stitches!

30 rows long

12 stitches wide

Finger puppets

Fold your knitted piece in half and sew the sides together. Sew up the top end and you have a perfect finger puppet.

Give your puppets faces using scraps of wool

Knitted purses

From knitted strips to handy bags.

Simple but useful, these little bags can be made to any size that suits you.

You will need:

- 4 mm knitting needles
- wool • embroidery needle
- buttons

Bag size

To make a larger or smaller bag, simply cast on more or fewer stitches and knit a longer or shorter strip.

1 Knit a strip

Sew the end in as shown on page 22.

Knit this strip

Cast on 15 stitches and keep knitting until your strip is 15 cm (6 in) long.

Sew the end in as shown on page 22.

2 Stitch it up

This will form the flap of the bag.

Sew up the sides with wool.

Fold the bottom of the bag up, as shown, leaving a flap.

3 Make a loop

1. Pass a threaded needle through the centre of the flap.

Don't pull it all the way through.

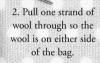

2. Pull one strand of wool through so the wool is on either side of the bag.

3. Knot the two strands together to make the loop.

Bring your purse alive by giving it a face. Glue on felt shapes or sew buttons for eyes.

Make a long cord to hang the bag round your neck.

Sew on a button to keep the bag shut.

Handy tip
Use your knitting doll cords (page 12) to make a strap. Put the end of the cord just inside the top of the bag and sew into place.

Krazy knits

Knit simple strips and use them to create your own zany friends.

Sew in strand as shown on page 22.

You will need:
• 4 mm knitting needles
• wool • felt scraps • fabric glue
• knitted cords • embroidery needle
• soft-toy stuffing

Fill up with stuffing.

Cast on 12 stitches.
Knit to length of 13 cm (5 in).

Fold the strip in half and sew up the sides leaving the top open.

1 Knit a strip

2 Fold it in half

3 Stuff it

Sew up the opening.

4 Sew it up

5 Give it a face

Cut out some shapes and glue them on.

Fabric glue
Cut some face shapes out of felt and glue them in place with fabric glue.

Legs and tails
Use cords from the knitting doll project (page 12) and stitch them on as legs and tails.

Cute cat

Krazy Kat

All-arms alien

Krazy Kat
To make Krazy Kat, knit a longer strip 23 cm (9 in) and follow the steps as before. Give him a head by tying a piece of wool around him then pulling it in tight.

Owls

Knitted pals

Short of soft toys?

Ted sits and knits a pal or two to play with him – and so could you!

Bobble hat

Easy knitting

Once you get the hang of knitting, you can make lots of different things. All the knitted projects in this book are made from squares and rectangles only – this makes them really easy! Start off with Ted, move onto his pals, then knit them all scarves and bobble hats.

Off we go...

Making Ted

Knit five pieces, sew them up, stuff them, and join them together. Hello Te

1

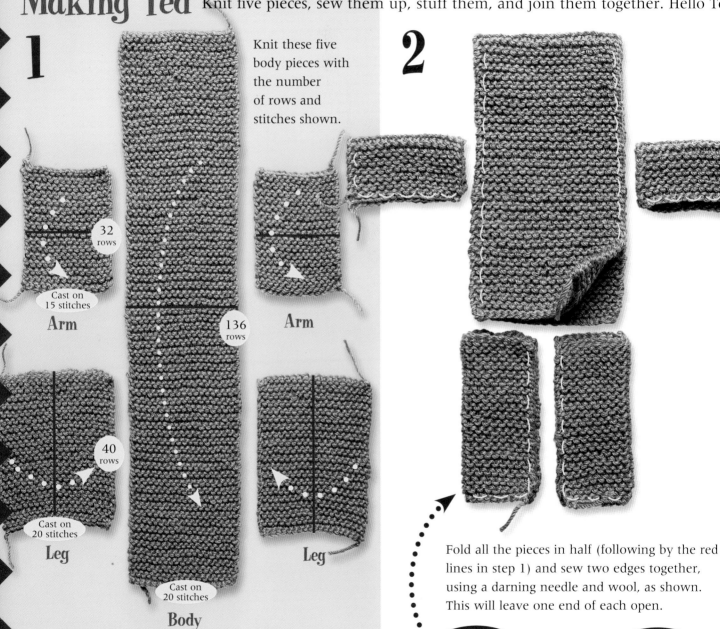

Knit these five body pieces with the number of rows and stitches shown.

32 rows

Cast on 15 stitches

Arm

136 rows

Arm

40 rows

Cast on 20 stitches

Leg

Leg

Cast on 20 stitches

Body

YOU WILL NEED...

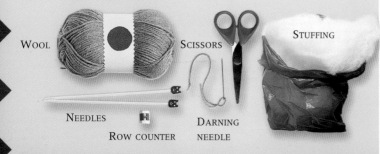

WOOL   SCISSORS   STUFFING

NEEDLES

ROW COUNTER   DARNING NEEDLE

2

Fold all the pieces in half (following by the red lines in step 1) and sew two edges together, using a darning needle and wool, as shown. This will leave one end of each open.

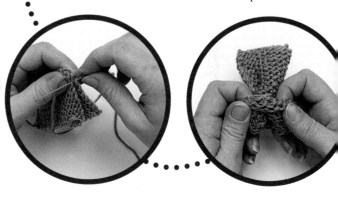

Run Ted, run!

3

Turn each piece inside out and stuff them. Sew up the end of each knitted piece.

4

Now sew the arms and legs to the body. Make sure you put them in the right place. You don't want a wonky Ted!

Use buttons for my eyes and nose.

Tie a bow under my chin to give me a neck.

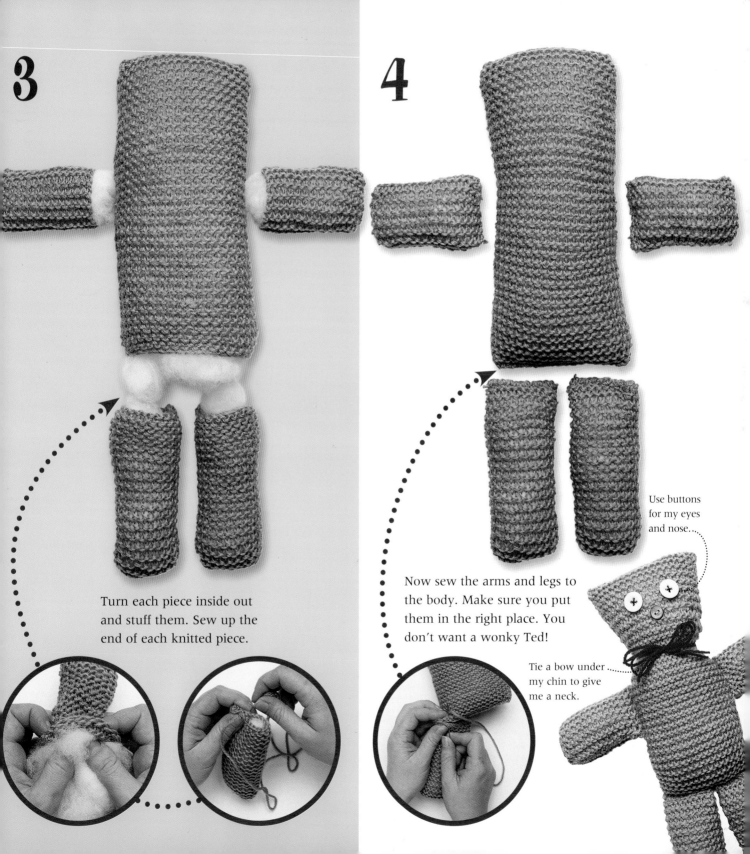

Ted's friends

You can't just make Ted, you need to make Ted's friends too. And what happens if they get cold? Knit them scarves and bobble hats of course!

Make a friend for Ted

Ted's friend is very easy because he has wibbly-wobbly arms and legs.

26 rows

72 rows

Cast on 5 stitches

Arm

Body

Cast on 16 stitches

40 rows

Cast on 5 stitches

Leg

Making friends

Knit the five body pieces, as shown. Fold the body in half, sew up two sides, turn it inside out, and stuff it – just like you did with Ted. Then sew up the body and attach the arms and legs.

Beanie hats

Everyone needs a hat.

Hat making

Ted's friend wants a hat. To make one, cas on 34 stitches and kn 20 rows. Fold in half, as above, and sew th top and sides togethe Pop it on and turn up the bottom.

Sew on old button or beads for the eyes and nose.

A pom-pom for the hat

Cut out two discs from thin card. Cut a hole in the middle of each one.

5 cm (2 in) across

Put the discs together and tie a piece of wool around them.

Wind the wool around and around through the middle and over the top. Stop when the discs are covered.

Use different colours.

Put a pair of scissors between the discs and snip the wool all around.

Tie a piece of wool tightly around the pom-pom.

Take away the card discs and fluff it up!

A fringe for the scarf

Knit Ted's long scarf as shown and finish it off nicely with a fringe.

Double up a piece of wool and pull it up through the hole.

A crochet needle is the best needle to use for this.

Push a needle through the scarf above the first row.

Take the two ends, bring them up through the loop and pull down firmly to make a fringe. Repeat along the row.

140 rows

Cast on 12 stitches

Ted's hat

Ted's cosy hat is made by casting on 66 stitches and knitting 46 rows. Turn it up and finish it off with a bright pom-pom. Once you can make Ted's scarf and hat, why not try making full-size ones for yourself or your friends.

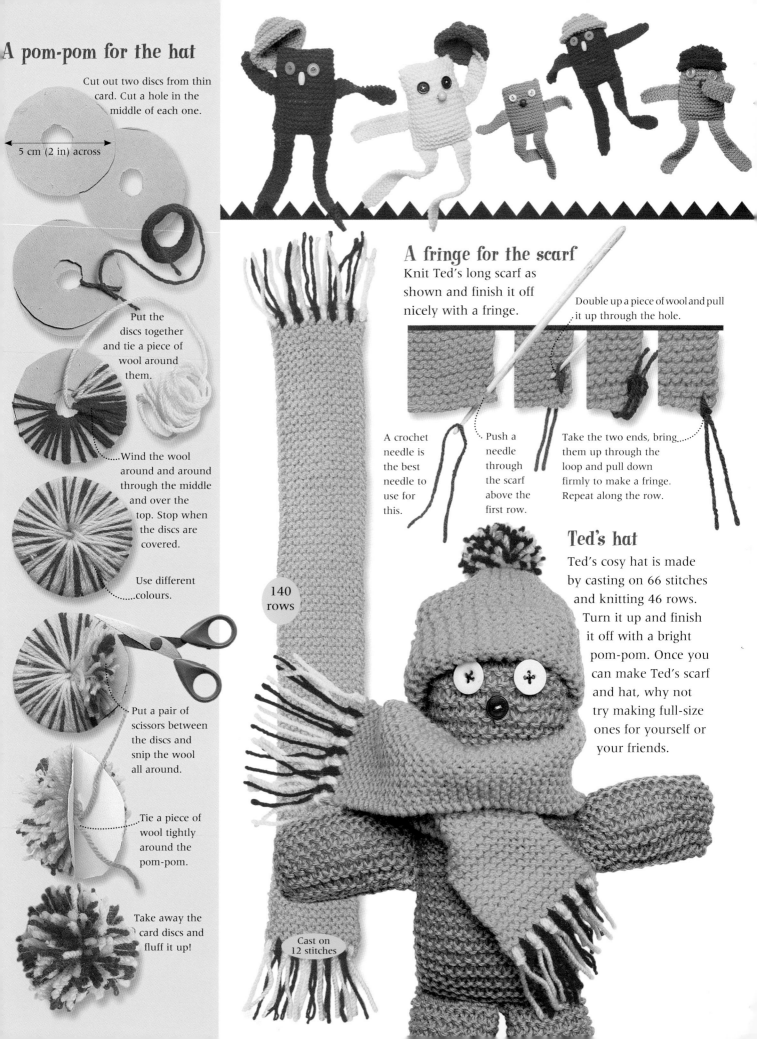

Woolly hats

A hat for you and a hat for Dolly!

1 Knit a strip

Cast on 16 stitches and knit to 20 cm (8 in) in length.

Use 4 mm needles for Dolly's hat.

Stitch the end back into the strip (see page 22).

You will need:
- knit a strip (see how to knit on page 20)
- embroidery needle
- felt flowers and pom-poms (for decoration)
- sewing needle and thread

2 Fold it in half

Sew the two edges together.

Knot the end of the yarn.

Sew running stitch around the top edge of the hat.

3 Gather one end of the hat

Pull the yarn tight to gather up the opening.

Sew backwards and forwards over the gathers to keep them together.

4 Secure the hat top

Felt flowers on page 86.

See how to make pom-poms on page 39.

Cut out felt shapes.

Sew the decorations to the hat with a sewing needle and thread.

5 Ready to decorate

Use 6 mm needles for your hat.

A hat for you

Follow the steps for Dolly's hat – just make yours bigger! Using 6 mm needles, cast on 30 stitches and knit to 50 cm (20 in) in length. Finish off the hat in the same way as Dolly's, then decorate.

Knit another strip to make Dolly a cosy scarf.

Pom-poms

Find out how to make pom-poms on page 39. To attach them to your hats, simply sew with a needle and thread. To make small pom-poms, cut small card discs about 5 cm (2 in).

Big knitting!

Big needles – big difference!
Try them and see.

4 mm needle

15 mm needle

How to use
Use large needles in the same way as small ones. And remember – the thinner the yarn, the looser the knit will be.

You will need:
• 15 mm big needles
• 200 gm ball of double-knit yarn

Pom-poms

You will need:
• two discs of card
• knitting yarn

Cut out two card discs 12 cm (5 in).

Put the two discs together and wrap the yarn around and around the card.

Pinch the middle. Slip the scissors between the discs and cut the yarn.

Slide a piece of yarn between the discs. Wrap it around the cut wool.

Pull the yarn tight and knot the ends together.

Pull off the pieces of card.

Big scarf

Make your knitting long enough for a scarf and finish it off with pom-poms.

To attach a pom-pom, gather up the end of the scarf and sew on the pom-pom using an embroidery needle and same-coloured wool.

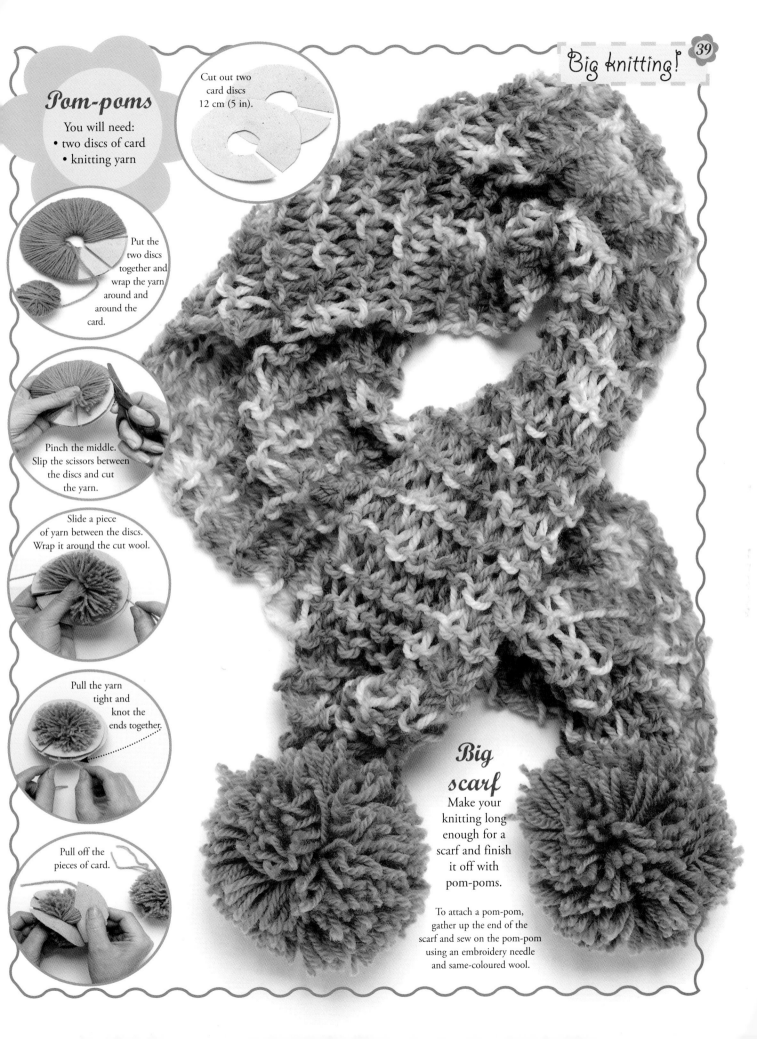

Fun with Wool

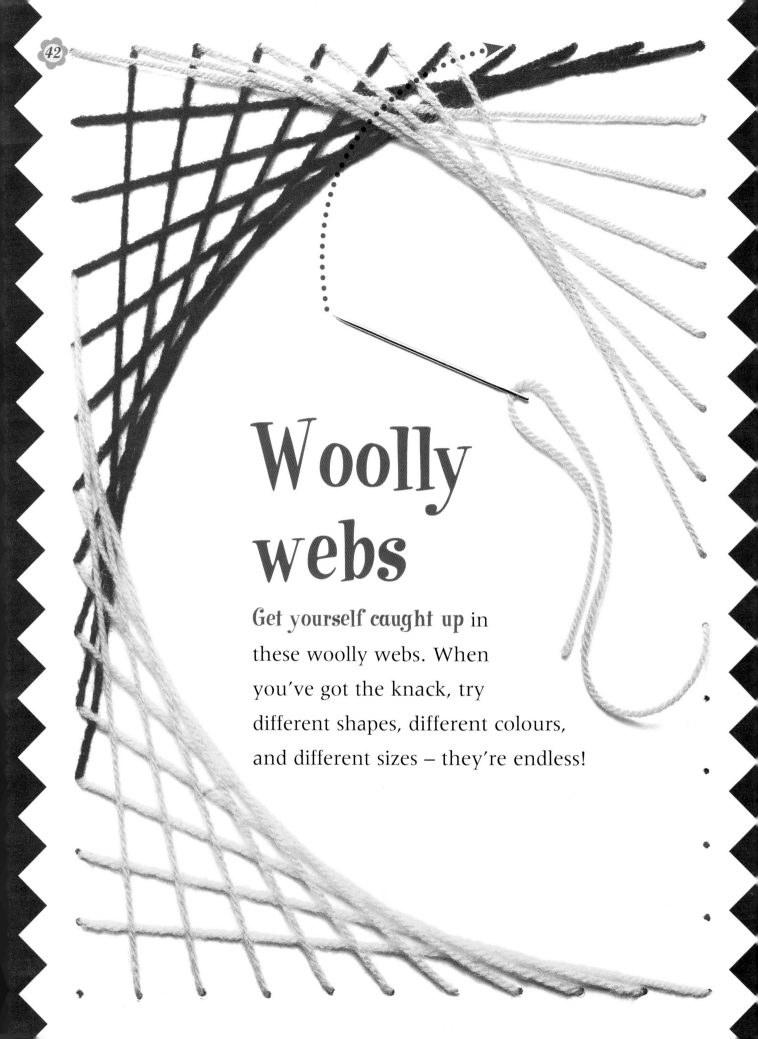

Woolly webs

Get yourself caught up in these woolly webs. When you've got the knack, try different shapes, different colours, and different sizes – they're endless!

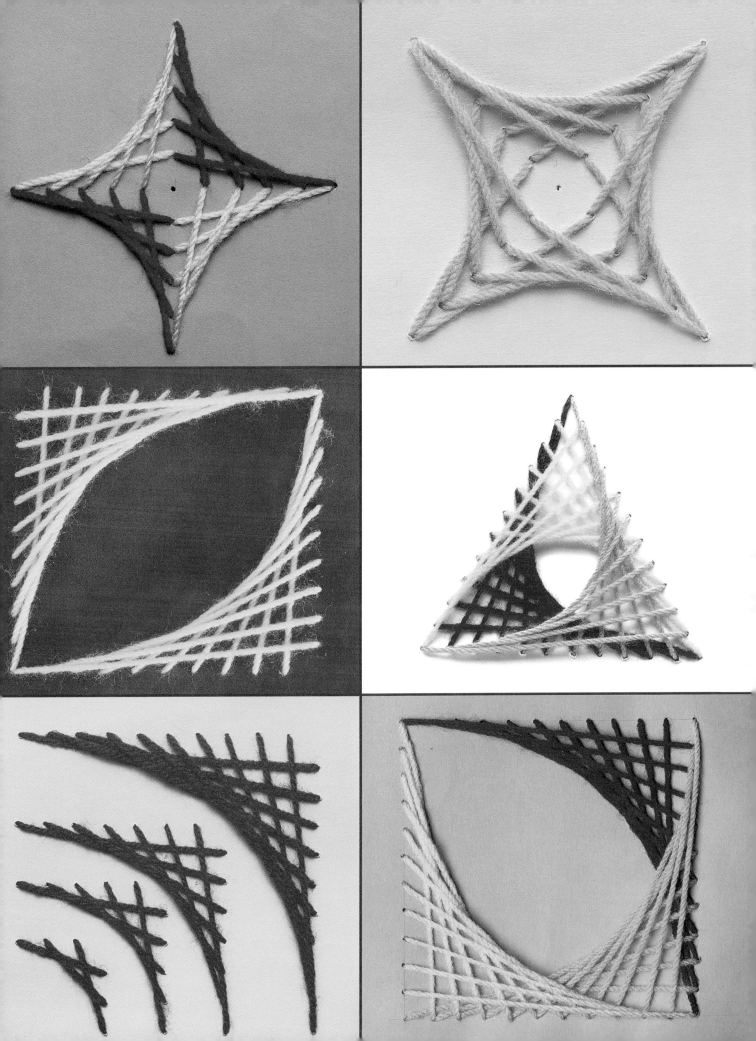

WEAVING KIT

WOOL

WOOL AND DARNING NEEDLE

THICK PAPER OR THIN CARD

SCISSORS

PENCIL

RULER

SET SQUARE

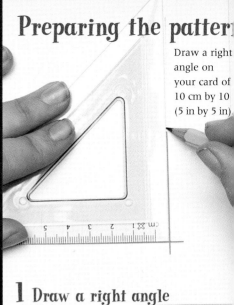

Preparing the patter

Draw a right angle on your card of 10 cm by 10 (5 in by 5 in)

1 Draw a right angle

Weaving tips

• Use thick paper or thin card. If the paper is too thin it will rip when you pull the thread through.

• For large patterns use wool, but for smaller designs lighter thread is best.

• When you get the hang of it, try using different coloured wool. When you are really good, try different patterns, such as the ones on the previous page.

• The most important thing is to EXPERIMENT and HAVE FUN.

Try the diamond design

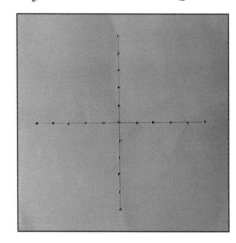

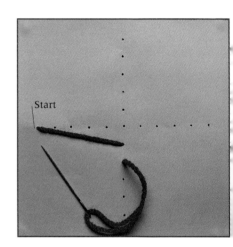

Start

The more holes you make the bigger the pattern will be...

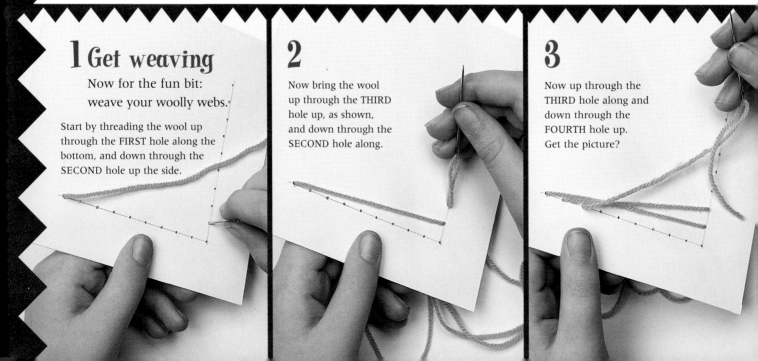

1 Get weaving

Now for the fun bit: weave your woolly webs.

Start by threading the wool up through the FIRST hole along the bottom, and down through the SECOND hole up the side.

2

Now bring the wool up through the THIRD hole up, as shown, and down through the SECOND hole along.

3

Now up through the THIRD hole along and down through the FOURTH hole up. Get the picture?

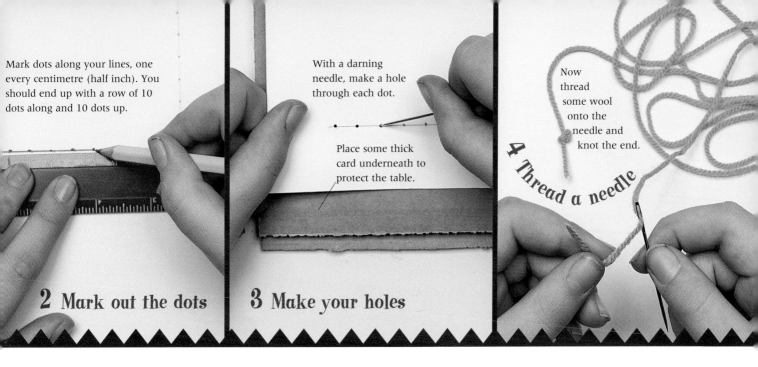

Mark dots along your lines, one every centimetre (half inch). You should end up with a row of 10 dots along and 10 dots up.

2 Mark out the dots

With a darning needle, make a hole through each dot.

Place some thick card underneath to protect the table.

3 Make your holes

Now thread some wool onto the needle and knot the end.

4 Thread a needle

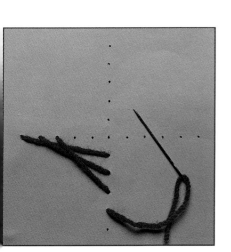
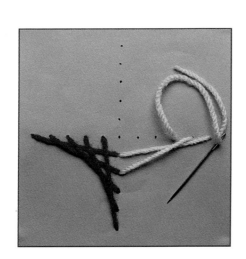
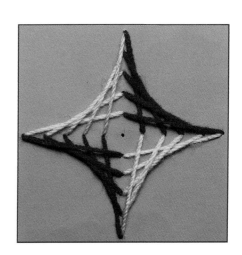

...and remember, you can use each hole more than once. Go on, weave a giant web!

4

Carry on weaving in this pattern until you have no more holes to fill.

5

The last hole you use should be the top one, so thread down through it and stop.

6

Turn the card over, tie a knot as close to the last stitch as possible, and trim the end of the wool.

Get weaving

wonderful webs in rainbow colours.

Paper plate

wool

A paper plate and scraps of wool create a rainbow web to brighten up your day.

To weave a web
You will need

- A paper plate or a circle of ca
- Scraps of wool
- Darning needle

1

Draw out a zig-zag edge around the plate and cut out the triangles.

2

knot

Loop the wool around two opposite spikes, making sure they cross in the middle and tie a knot in the centre.

3

Keep crossing the wool from spike to spike, making sure the wool crosses through the middle.

The wool will go around this one next.

4

Keep going backwards and forwards across the plate.

5

Turn your plate over and it should look like this. Tie the end of the wool into a knot.

6

Thread a piece of wool onto a needle. From the middle, weave the needle between the strands.

It will look odd at first but after about six rows, it will even out.

7

As you weave, make sure you pull it tight into the middle.

8

Knot a new piece of wool to the last one and just keep on weaving.

use up your old scraps

Continue weaving different colours until there's no more room.

keep on weaving

Looms are frames used for weaving fabric. Make a simple loom and have a go at creating a piece of fabric and then start to weave anything you can find!

Home-made loom

A shoebox lid is ideal. Cut the same number of slits on opposite ends then thread wool backwards and forwards.

1

Ask an Adult to cut the slits, they may need to use a sharp knife.

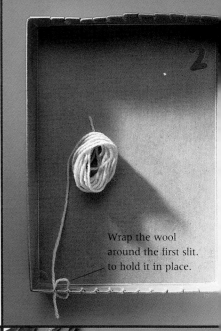

2

Wrap the wool around the first slit to hold it in place.

3

Keep going up and down.

4

Thread the wool above and below the main strands and forward and back.

Now try weaving other things that you can find.

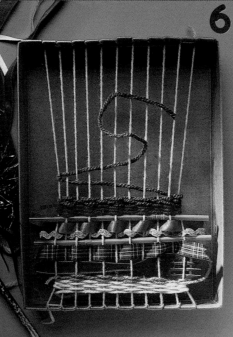

6

Weave and weave until you reach the top.

Ribbon

Wool

Plastic
Knife

Pencil

Tinsel

Straw

Fancy
Ribbon

Plastic
Fork

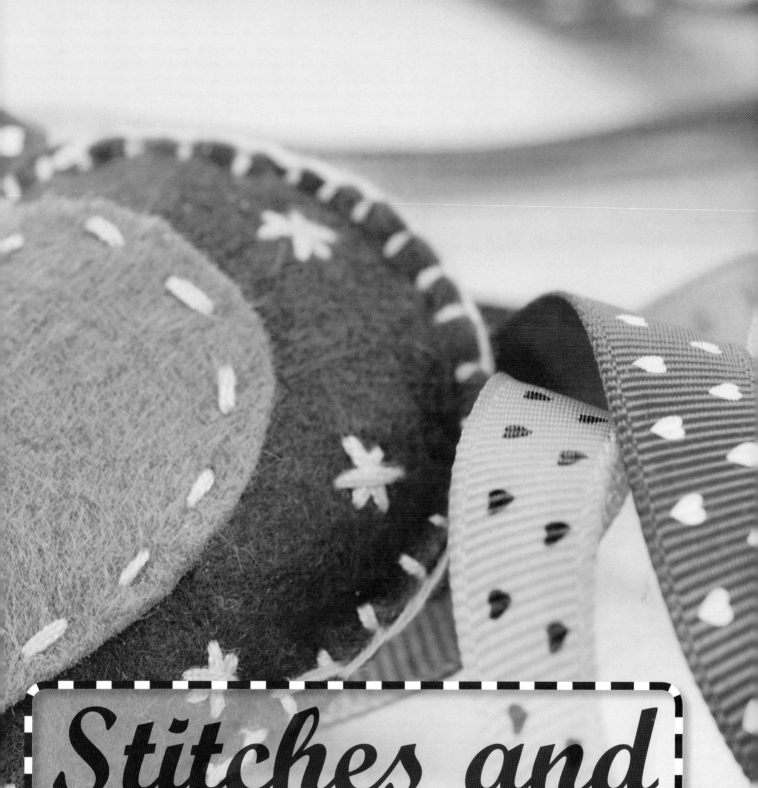

Stitches and Embroidery

Made by Me Workboxes

A lunch box or mini suitcase is ideal.

Pack away your bits and bobs.

Before you go shopping for a workbox, try looking around your home first. Customizing a box that you find is much more fun!

Handy tip

Decide what you want to store in your box, then choose one that will fit your equipment. Decorate it with ribbons and trimmings to make it look like a sewing box.

Glue on colourful ribbons and trimmings

Stick a piece of fabric to the lid of the box to hold pins and needles.

Use smaller boxes as trays inside the case to hold cotton and threads.

Workbox ideas

- **Snack containers** – tall tubes with pop-on lids are very good for storing your knitting needles.

- **Egg boxes** – they have a ready-made lid and are good for all the little bits you need, like pins and needles.

- **Jam jars** – collect jars and fill them with different things like buttons and threads. Decorate them using material and fabric glue.

A small container with a pop-on lid

Jam jar

Turn the jar lid into a pin cushion.

Thread jar, button jar, pin jar – jars for everything!

You will need:

- scissors • fabric glue
- fabric • felt • ribbons and trimmings • bits and bobs, such as egg boxes, jam jars and buttons

Egg boxes

Egg boxes are great because they have compartments inside them.

Attach felt flowers with fabric glue.

Snack boxes

These boxes are wrapped in fabric that's glued in place.

Embroidery

Learn the embroidery stitches and you can decorate clothes, cushions – whatever you like!

Scissors

Cotton fabric

Tapestry canvas

Aida fabric for cross-stitch

Rounded needle

Pointed needle

Fabrics

You can do embroidery on all kinds of fabrics – from jeans to T-shirts. The fabrics shown here are cotton, (which has a close weave), tapestry canvas, and Aida, (which has large holes and is good for cross-stitch).

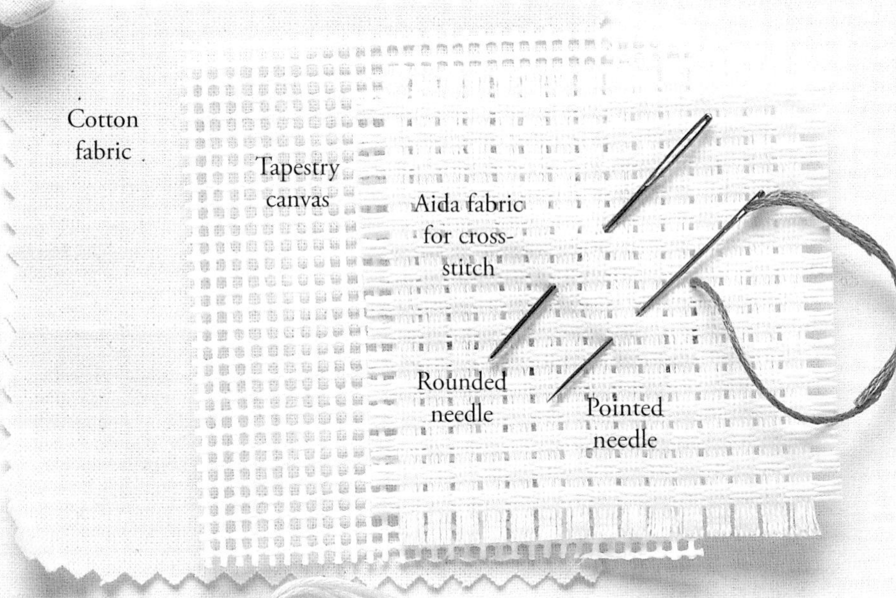

Needles

Embroidery needles have large, long eyes with pointed ends or rounded ends. Use the pointed end when working with close-weave fabric like cotton, and the rounded end when doing tapestry or cross-stitch.

Threads

Threads used in embroidery are sold in skeins. They are usually made from cotton or wool.

Embroidery thread

This thread is made of cotton and can be used for most embroidery stitches. Suitable for fine-weave fabrics and Aida.

Tapestry wool

This thread is made of wool and is used for tapestry and coarse-weave fabrics.

Embroidery thread

Tapestry wool

A frame helps you to hold the fabric in place.

This fabric is calico. It's lightweight cotton and is cheap to buy.

Screw tightens large hoop.

Frames

Frames are used to stretch the fabric, so the area you are working on is flat and easy to handle.

Frames have two hoops – one inside the other. Separate the hoops and place the fabric over the smaller hoop. Then place the larger hoop over the top and tighten the screw.

Plastic hoop stretches over a smaller hoop.

Embroidery

What is it?
Embroidery is stitching that enables you to create pictures and patterns. It can be used to decorate all kinds of fabrics using yarns and threads.

A pin cushion keeps needles safe.

Practise your design on paper first.

Aida is available in different colours.

Stitch directory

These are the stitches that you use throughout the book.

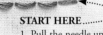

Stitching tip
Try and keep your stitches even and neat.

Running stitch

This creates a dotted line – simply push the needle in and out of the fabric. Start by making a knot in the end of the thread.

2. Push the needle down and up through the fabric and pull to make a stitch.

START HERE
1. Pull the needle up through the fabric to the knot.

Backstitch

This makes a continuous line of stitches, but unlike running stitch, you go back to fill the gap between the stitch each time.

2. Start as if you are doing running stitch, then take the needle back to the end of the last stitch.

3. Bring the needle back up here.

START HERE
1. Pull the needle up through the fabric to the knot.

Lazy daisy stitch

This pretty stitch is very useful for embroidery decoration. Draw out your daisy design first in light pencil, then follow the lines with your stitches.

2. Now bring it up through another petal until you have finished the flower.

1. Tie a knot in your thread and pull it up through the beginning of a petal and down at the end.

Chain stitch

This is a very useful decorating stitch – great for flower stems and leaves. You may need to practise the stitch to get it just right.

1. Tie a knot in the thread and pull it up through the fabric.

2. Now push the needle back down next to the thread.

3. Don't pull it tight, leave a little loop.

4. Now bring the needle up through the loop and pull the thread through.

5. Repeat stages 1 to 4. Keep the stitches as even as possible.

Practise chain stitch on a curved line so you can make shapes.

Blanket stitch

This stitch is good for making neat, decorative edges and for sewing one piece of fabric to another.

1. Tie a knot in the thread and pull the needle up through the fabric.

2. Push the needle back through next to the stitch and up below it, making sure the loose end is caught as shown.

3. Push the needle down and up again so it is the same size as the previous stitch, catching the loose thread again.

4. Repeat these steps to make more loops.

Cross-stitch

You can make whole pictures using cross-stitch (see page 66).

Draw out crosses in light pencil on your fabric.

Sew a line of crosses from left to right in one direction...

... then finish them off by sewing back the other way.

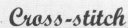

Decorate a T-shirt

Embroidery thread

Flatten the end of the thread to help it go through the eye of the needle.

Knot the end.

Finish stitching

On the back of the fabric, push the needle through the loop of the last stitch.

Pull the thread tight and repeat to make it secure.

You need to use an embroidery needle with a big eye.

Use the stitches on this page to jazz up your T-shirt. And try decorating bags, jeans pockets, and any other clothes too.

Blanket-stitch edging

Blanket stitch the edge of the T-shirt using the seam as a guide.

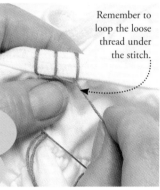

Remember to loop the loose thread under the stitch.

Draw on designs

Practise drawing your designs onto paper first. Then copy the pattern onto your T-shirt in pencil – this will disappear when you wash your shirt.

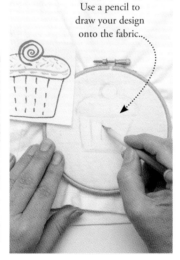

Use a pencil to draw your design onto the fabric.

OR sandwich carbon paper between the fabric and the drawing.

Trace over your design to transfer it onto the fabric.

Stitch your design following the marks on the fabric.

Sew on a button

Push the needle up through the spot where you want the button to be.

Then thread the button onto the needle and drop it down the thread.

Sew down through the other button hole and the fabric, then up again through the first hole.

Repeat this five more times.

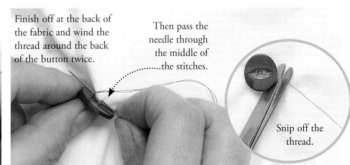

Finish off at the back of the fabric and wind the thread around the back of the button twice.

Then pass the needle through the middle of the stitches.

Snip off the thread.

Picture stitches

Transfer your doodles onto fabric. Then embroider over the lines to make pretty stitched pictures.

You will need:
- embroidery frame
- skeins of embroidery silk
- embroidery needle
- fabric

Work out your design on paper first.

Put the fabric in the frame.

Copy your design onto the fabric.

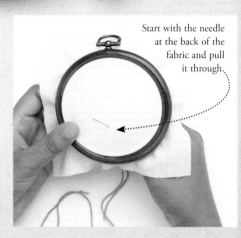

Start with the needle at the back of the fabric and pull it through.

Pull the thread through to the knot.

Knot the end of the thread.

Stitch along the pencil lines, (see page 56 to see how to do running stitch).

To finish off a colour, Turn the frame over...

... slip the thread back through the last stitches, and cut off the end.

Begin and end colours in the same way.

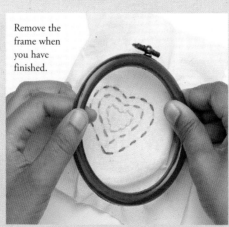

Remove the frame when you have finished.

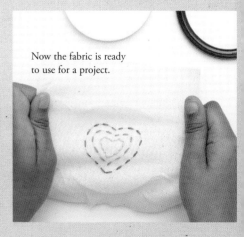

Now the fabric is ready to use for a project.

Backstitch

Lazy daisy stitch

Running
stitch

**Stitch
directory**
Go to page 56 to
learn how to do these
fancy stitches.

Chain stitch

Cross-stitch

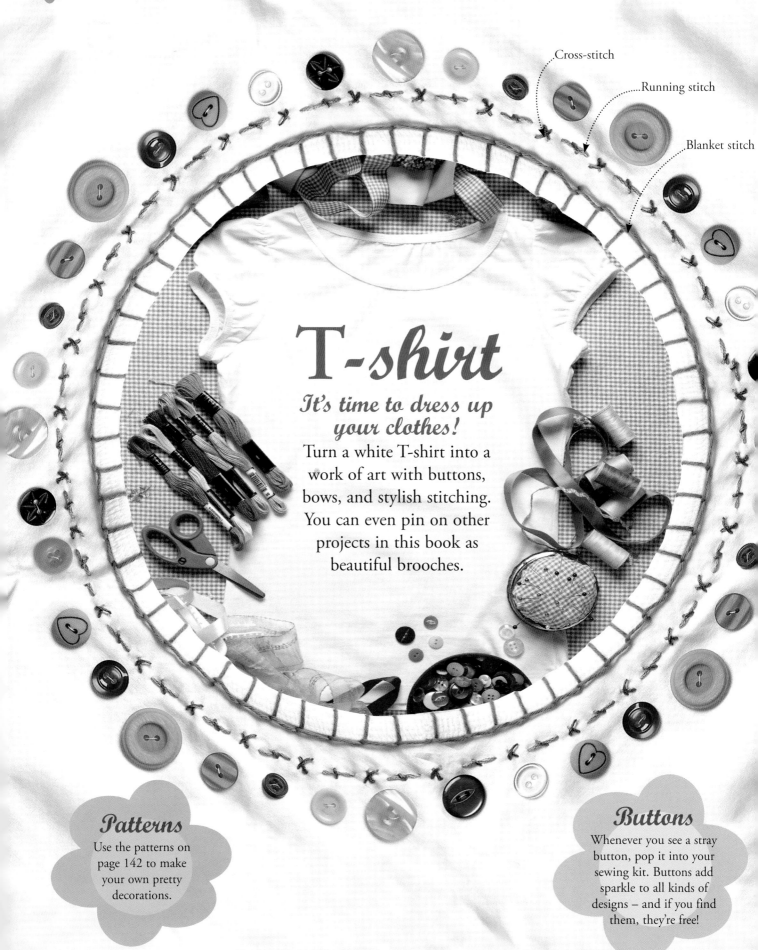

Cross-stitch

Running stitch

Blanket stitch

T-shirt

It's time to dress up your clothes!

Turn a white T-shirt into a work of art with buttons, bows, and stylish stitching. You can even pin on other projects in this book as beautiful brooches.

Patterns

Use the patterns on page 142 to make your own pretty decorations.

Buttons

Whenever you see a stray button, pop it into your sewing kit. Buttons add sparkle to all kinds of designs – and if you find them, they're free!

xx T-shirt xx

Cross-stitch

Blanket stitch

Chain stitch

Blanket stitch

Cup cakes (see page 118)

Running stitch

Pocket locket (see page 82)

Handy tip
Work out your designs on paper before you sew them onto your T-shirt. (See pages 56 and 57 for stitch decorations.)

Running stitch

The ABC of cross-stitch

When you've perfected your A, B, Cs,
put your letters together to make a name,
write a message, or even draw a
cross-stitch picture.

Cross-stitch

Simple samplers are as easy as A, B, C. Criss, cross, criss, cross, and create pictures.

Following guide lines

• Draw out the area you want to sew as small squares – each square is one cross-stitch.

• To keep your letters the same size, base them on the same number of squares across and up – for example, 4 squares across and 7 squares up.

• Remember, the curving part of a letter still has to be drawn using the squares.

Don't make the line too dark or it will show through your stitches.

Pencil

Binka fabric • *Darning needle*

You will need

BINKA FABRIC • The large holes make it easy to see where to sew.

THREAD• Use anything from fine silk thread to thick wool.

NEEDLE • A darning needle is easy to thread and fits through the holes.

PENCIL • To mark out the squares.

Embroidery thread

Scissors

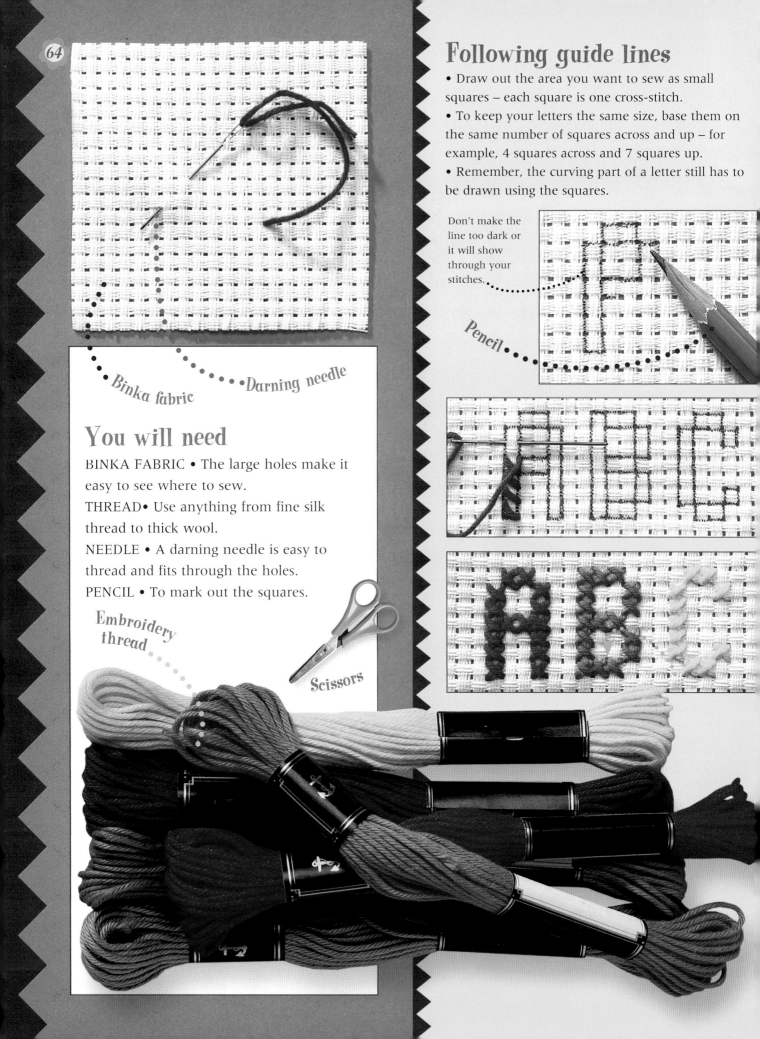

Single stitch

For one stitch use a short length of thread and don't forget to knot the end.

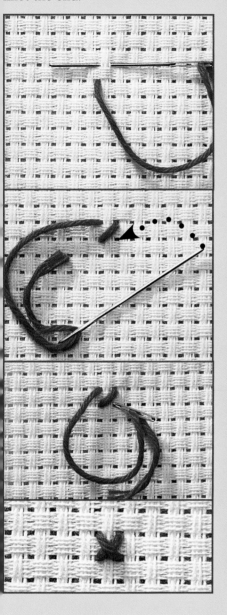

Stitches in a row

To make a row, sew a few stitches, then go back the other way.

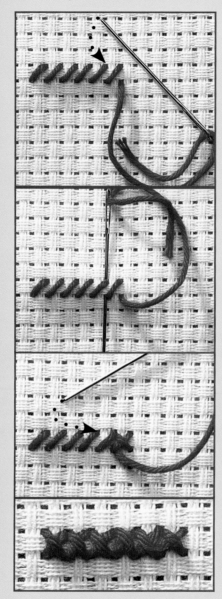

A·B·C cross-stitch letter squares

Once you have learnt how to cross-stitch, experiment with different patterns and colours. To start, try stitching single letters. Cut a square of fabric about 18 holes by 18 holes. Draw on your design in pencil, and stitch away.

Try fringing the edges of your work by pulling away the first few strands of the fabric along the edge.

Back view and finishing off

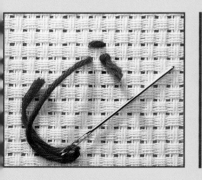

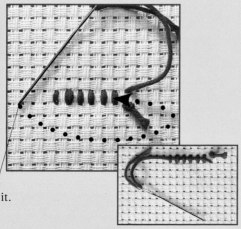

Finish a stitch on the back and thread it through other nearby stitches to secure it.

Cross-stitch

Crisscross, crisscross.

Cross-stitch is so easy and as long as you keep the designs simple, it will look good enough to hang on a wall! You can even write in cross-stitch.

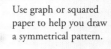

1 Draw a picture

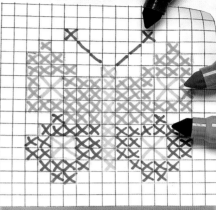

Use graph or squared paper to help you draw a symmetrical pattern.

Colour in your picture.

2 Collect your materials

Aida fabric

Embroidery frame

Embroidery needle with a rounded end

Embroidery thread

3 Transfer your design

Put the fabric into the frame.

Use a pencil to draw your design onto the fabric.

4 Start stitching

See page 56 for cross-stitch instructions.

Stitch over your design.

Stitch in rows as much as possible.

5 Finish it off

Remove the frame and straighten out the fabric...

...or use the embroidery frame as a picture frame.

Gather up the fabric at the back and sew in place.

Sampler

A sampler is a piece of fabric that you practise on. Experiment with different sized cross-stitches and different coloured threads. With this type of fabric you don't always need a picture frame.

When you have finished, fray the edge of the fabric to make it look pretty.

Little mats

Samplers make lovely little mats too. When you've finished stitching, glue them onto felt.

Pixel pix

Tapestries are made up of
little squares, just like pixels on a computer. Try making pictures where each stitch is like a pixel.

Tapestry wool

Sew a picture

Draw a picture on squared paper, making sure you use the squares as the outline of the shape.

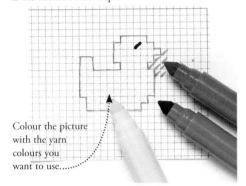

Colour the picture with the yarn colours you want to use.

Carefully transfer the colours onto some tapestry canvas.

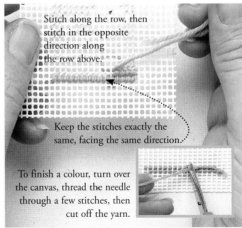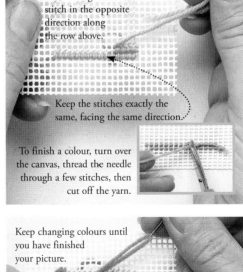

Each stitch will be stitched at an angle.

Embroidery needle with a rounded end

Tapestry canvas

Cut a length of yarn, thread the needle, and knot the end.

Pull the needle up through the canvas then down through the diagonal stitch above to the right.

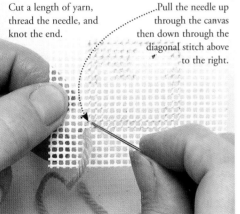

Stitch along the row, then stitch in the opposite direction along the row above.

Keep the stitches exactly the same, facing the same direction.

To finish a colour, turn over the canvas, thread the needle through a few stitches, then cut off the yarn.

Graph or squared paper

Begin the next colour working along the rows as before.

Keep changing colours until you have finished your picture.

Scissors

It's a gift
Make a pixel picture for a special present. You could frame one, or turn one into a brooch or key ring.

To practise, try stitching patterns rather than pictures.

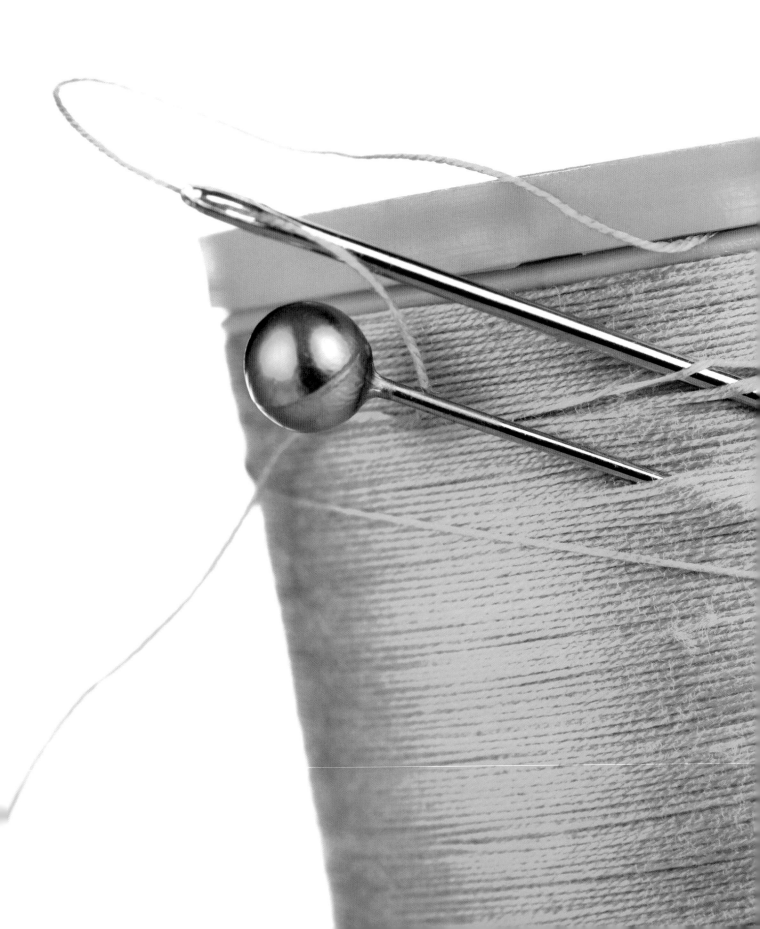

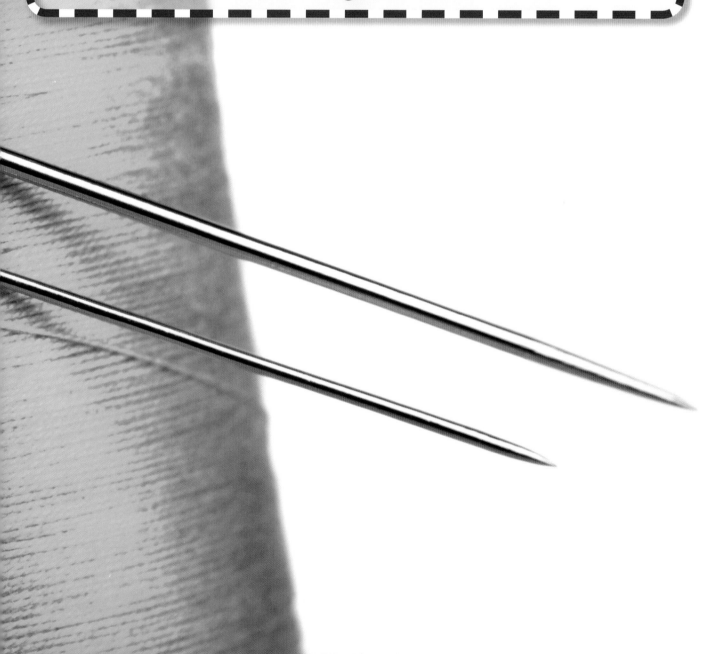

Sewing Projects

Pins

Sewing

Here you'll find out how to make bags and pouches, and how to make fabulous fabric jewellery too!

Safety pins

Buttons for decorating and fastening

Pins

Pins help hold fabrics together and safety pins are useful for threading ribbons.

Felt

Use pinking shears to stop the edges of the fabric from fraying.

Corduroy

Fabric

The projects in this book mainly use lightweight cotton and felt. Felt is good as it doesn't fray at the edges. There are other fabrics to choose from too, including corduroy.

Cotton

Needles

Sewing needles are small and thin with a round eye. Choose a medium-sized needle for your work.

Scissors

Use a tape measure to check your fabric is the right size.

Tape measure

Needle threader

Sewing thread

This is made of cotton and can be used for all the sewing projects here. Use a needle threader if you have trouble pushing the thread through the eye.

Cotton thread

Trimmings

Trimmings, such as ribbons and lace edging, finish off your projects perfectly.

Ribbons and lace

Pin cushion

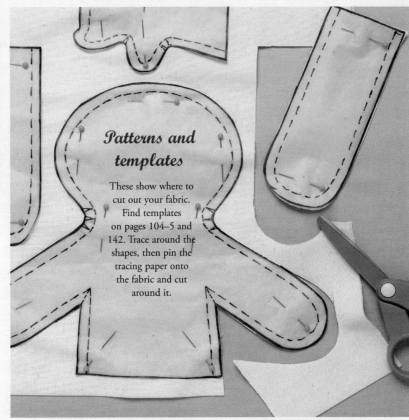

Patterns and templates

These show where to cut out your fabric. Find templates on pages 104–5 and 142. Trace around the shapes, then pin the tracing paper onto the fabric and cut around it.

Sewing

What is sewing? Sewing is stitching to decorate or connect together pieces of fabric. When you sew you can make toys, bags, and clothes.

Fun with felt

Felt is great to use as decoration and comes in all sorts of different colours.

Sewing

Pinking shears

These scissors don't just give a decorative edge to your fabric...

... the zig-zag edge stops the fabric fraying too.

Pouches

Bags for everything - from little ones to hold your hair clips to big ones for your shoes.

1 Cut out the fabric

Fold the fabric over by 13 mm ($\frac{1}{2}$ in).

Sew the fold down using running stitch.

As a guide, cut out a piece of fabric 10 cm x 17 cm (4 in x 7 in).

You will need:
- cotton fabric (see steps for size)
- sewing thread
- needles and pins
- safety pin
- ribbon

2 Stitch it up

Fold edge.

Fold the fabric in half, right sides together, and pin in place.

Sew up the two edges using running stitch. Leave the top open.

3 Turn right side out

Turn the bag right side out.

Push the safety pin through the gap in the end.

Cut a piece of ribbon 30 cm (12 in) long.

Attach a safety pin to the end of the ribbon.

Handy pins

Attaching a safety pin to the end of the ribbon gives you something solid to guide through the fabric.

4 Cut the ribbon

5 Thread the ribbon

Work the pin around until it comes through the other side, then remove the pin.

Ribbon ties

When you have threaded the ribbon, tie the two ends together so they can't slip out. Push the material along the ribbon to close the bag.

Big bag

Cut a piece of fabric 50 cm x 25 cm (20 in x 10 in).

Medium bag

Cut a piece of fabric 40 cm x 20 cm (16 in x 8 in).

You could try

Stitch your friend's name on a bag and fill it with wrapped sweets. It'll make a perfect present!

Baby bag

Cut a piece of fabric 10 cm x 17 cm (4 in x 7 in).

Pirate Pete

Yo, ho, ho, it's a pirate's life for me! How would you like to be drawn, sewn, and stuffed? That's how I'm made.

Ship a'hoy!

Shiver me beanbags

This jolly pirate is stuffed full of rice. You can use dried food, such as lentils, popping corn, dried beans, or small pasta. Don't stuff it too full, however – it needs to be a bit floppy.

Follow the lines and dots

The hard line shows you where you cut the material, and the dotted line shows you where you sew.

Include these ears for cat shape.

Leave a space here to fill your toy.

YOU WILL NEED

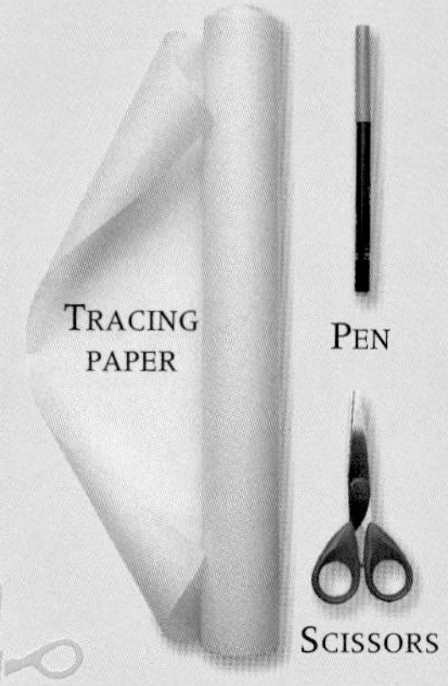

TRACING PAPER

PEN

SCISSORS

Pirate pattern

Sew along this line.

Cut out along this line.

Snip away these triangles from the material. This will help the shape to turn inside out neatly.

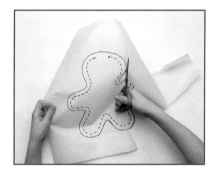

Place a piece of tracing paper over this page and draw around the outline you have chosen. Cut the shape out.

Cut straight along here for ghost or snowman shapes.

Meet the gang

"All aboard the Jolly Roger!" shouts Pete. He couldn't sail his ship without his trusted beanbag crew. "Hoist the sails, raise the anchor, we're off to find hidden treasure!"

Beanbag tips

Pete's pattern can be used to make the crew too. Just add extra ears for the animals, woolly plaits for the girls, and leave out the legs for the ghosts and snowman.

Throw together Pete

Pirate Pete is ready to be cut out

for a life on the high seas. Use the template from page 77 to make him and go on to throw together his whole crew. "Ha, ha, me hearties!"

YOUR PIRATE KIT

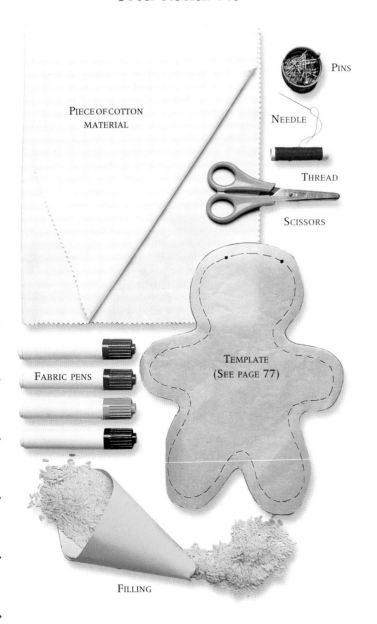

PIECE OF COTTON MATERIAL

PINS

NEEDLE

THREAD

SCISSORS

FABRIC PENS

TEMPLATE
(SEE PAGE 77)

FILLING

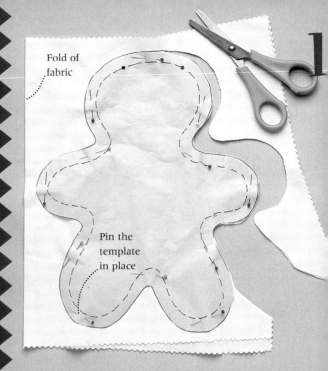

Fold of fabric

Pin the template in place

Cut out the shape

Fold a piece of material in half. Lay your template o top. Cut it out. You will now have two Pete shapes.

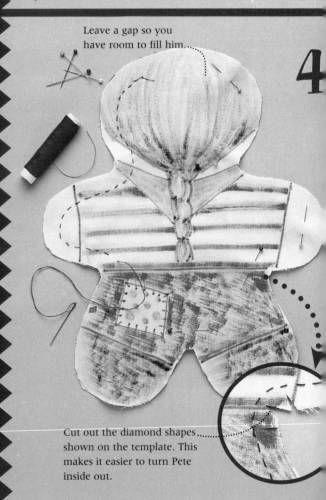

Leave a gap so you have room to fill him

4

Cut out the diamond shapes shown on the template. This makes it easier to turn Pete inside out.

Sew all the way around

Use small backstitches (see page 141) to sew around the pirate. Leave a small gap at the top.

Use fabric pens to colour Pirate Pete.

2

Draw Pirate Pete

Colour the front of Pete on one piece and draw the back of him on the other.

3

Pin the pieces together

Place the right sides of Pete together and pin them in place.

Turn the fabric through the gap in the stitching.

5

Curl a piece of paper into a tube funnel for easy filling.

When you have filled Pete, fold the open edges inwards, pin them together, and stitch the opening.

6

Turn him inside out

You should now see the right sides of Pete on the outside.

Fill him up

Fill up Pirate Pete with rice or beans, and sew him up!

Pocket lockets

More than just pretty pendants!
They are the perfect place to keep your keys. Just slide the felt sleeve up and down the ribbon to use or hide your key.

Try it out

You will need:
- felt shapes cut to size (use the patterns on page 142)
- skein of embroidery silk
- embroidery needle
- pins
- ribbon – long or short

Tie the ribbon into a big knot that won't slip through the felt sleeve.

Position the ribbon between the felt pieces.

Pin the felt and ribbon together.

Use blanket stitch (see page 56) to sew the back and front together. Make sure you don't sew through the ribbon.

Pull the sleeve up and down the ribbon to hide or show the key.

Cut two felt shapes for the key sleeve.

Cut some felt shapes for decoration.

Sew the shapes to the front felt piece.

Loop the ribbon through the key.

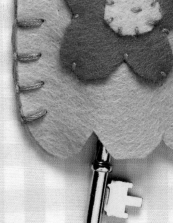

1 Sew on decoration

2 Sew up the sides

3 All done!

Dotty

Fancy stitches
Experiment with the embroidery stitches that you'll find earlier in the book.

Daisy

Owl

Key pendants
Make sure the ribbon is long enough to fit around your neck, or short enough to wear on your wrist.

Chimp

Hanging softies

Make a collection of mini padded shapes
and hang them absolutely everywhere!

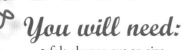

You will need:
- felt shapes cut to size (use the patterns on page 142)
- skeins of embroidery silk
- embroidery needle
- stuffing

Back shape

Front shape

Cut out some hearts

Decoration

Front only

Front and back

Sewing tip
Keep your stitches the same size and evenly spaced apart.

Decorate the front before attaching the back.

Join the front and the back together using blanket stitch (see page 56), leaving a small gap.

1 Sew on the decorations

2 Sew the hearts together

Fill the shape with stuffing – but not too full.

Sew up the gap and fasten off.

3 Stuff it

4 Stitch together.

Templates
Use the patterns on page 142 – or make up your own.

Hang up
Add embroidery silk
or a ribbon and you can
hang a softie anywhere –
on the Christmas tree,
a door knob...

Gift ideas
• *Brooch* - Sew a safety
pin to the back of a softie.
• *Key ring* - Attach your
softie to your key ring.
• *Necklace* - Use ribbon
to turn a softie into
something to wear.

Felt flowers

Pretty petals
are a perfect finish for a party
outfit. Pin them to hair clips,
hair bands, bangles,
and bags.

You will need:
- felt shapes cut to size (use the patterns on page 142)
- needle and sewing thread
- buttons

Make a flower

1. Make a petal-shaped template, then make five felt petals.

Draw around the card.

2. Cut out the petals.

3. Sew the petals together using running stitch (page 56).

Hair grips

Hair bands

4. Sew the last petal to the edge of the first one.

5. Pull the thread carefully to gather up the fabric petals.

6. Sew through the gathers to hold them together.

Finishing touches

1. Make another flower. Stitch through the flowers' centres.

2. Attach them by sewing on a button (see page 57).

3. Sew or glue onto a hair band, hair clip, or a bangle.

Handy tip

These flowers are a really handy way of using up your scraps. When you make a felt project, keep the little pieces to make lots of coloured flowers.

Fashion flowers

Use these fancy flowers to decorate your clothes and bags.

Bags of Ribbons

All the trimmings – collect up lots and lots of ribbon scraps and turn them into multi-coloured bags.

BAG BACK
Use a thick fabric
10 cm x 10 cm
(4 in x 4 in).

BAG FRONT use light cotton
10 cm x 10 cm (4 in x 4 in).

You will need:
- two squares of material – lightweight cotton for the front and heavier cotton for the back
- sewing thread
- needle and pins
- lots of ribbon scraps

Cut lots of pieces of ribbon the same width as the fabric.

1 Collect up the pieces

Sew the first ribbon at the bottom.

Fold over the top to make it neat and hem in place using little stitches.

Sew the last piece of ribbon over the folded edge.

Add lace and other trimmings as well.

2 Sew on the ribbon

3 Add some trimmings

Ribbons
Look out for ribbon on presents and packaging and start collecting it. Even small lengths can be used to decorate your projects.

Place the right sides together.

Sew round three sides using backstitch (see page 56).

Fold over the top to make it neat, then hem it.

4 Join the front and back

5 Turn right side out

Add a strap
Cut a piece of ribbon long enough to hang the bag from your shoulder. Sew it to the sides of the finished bag.

Ribbon strap

Big or small
The size of this bag is just a guide. You can make the bag as big or as little as you like. Decide what you want to carry around and make a bag to fit it.

You could use buttons to attach the strap.

Customize CUSHIONS

Whether you go for junk-filled bubble wrap or brilliant bows, colourful cacti or sparkling tinsel, rainbow stripes or zebra patterns, you can re-invent the cushion for your bedroom. Bright colours and cool designs will work wonders – they'll add life to an old chair, a dull corner, or a tired bed.

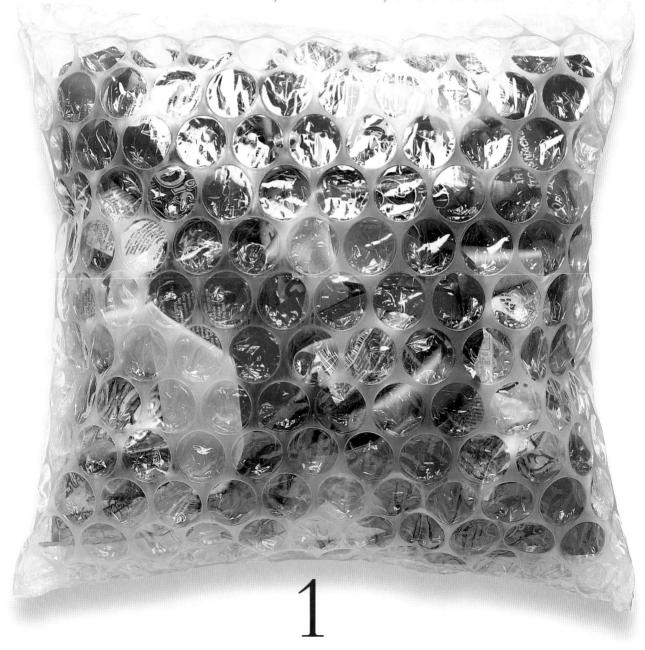

1

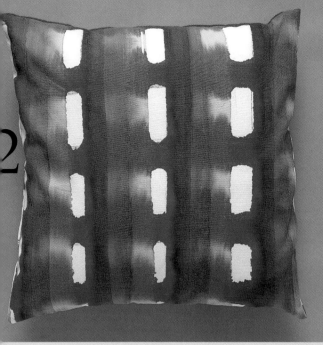

2

3

4

5

6

Customize Cushions

Making a cushion cover

You can customize a ready-made cushion cover, but if you want to make one of your own, here's how. Start by cutting out two pieces of fabric that are about 35 cm x 35 cm, or the size that will fit an existing cushion. Pin these together. Starting about 1.5 cm from the edge, sew the two pieces together. Leave a 25 cm space on one edge to allow room for the cushion. Trim off the corners, then turn the case inside out. Push in a cushion pad and neatly sew up the open edge.

Pin the fabric together with the right sides facing each other.

Cushion 1

Cushion covers don't need to be made from fabric, so why not experiment? Bubble wrap, for example, makes an unusual cushion. Cut out a long oblong piece – 30 cm x 60 cm is about the right size for a small cushion. Tape two of the open sides together, and then fill the cushion with empty crisp packets, sweet papers, fabric, or any other soft, colourful item you have around. Once the cushion is full, tape it up.

The piece of bubble wrap should be twice the width of the cushion you want to make.

Bring the sides to meet in the middle.

Use clear tape to stick the edges together.

Don't overfill the bag or the seams will split.

Fold over the open edges, and then seal with tape.

Use small, neat stitches to sew up the cushion.

Be careful not to trim the corners close to the stitches or you will make a hole.

Push the corners into points when you turn the case the right way out.

Make sure you don't tear the cover when you stuff it.

Use matching thread to sew the gap closed.

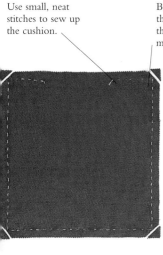

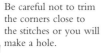

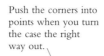

Use material with interesting textures.

Wrap the ribbon around the cushion as you would decorate a present.

Cushions 2 and 4

Use the fabric you designed using paint or dye to make colourful cushion covers. For an even brighter variation, add a ribbon, tied in a simple bow.

Cushion 3

Cut out shapes from scrap material and glue them onto the fabric. Use bold stitches to help hold the fabric in place – they can become part of the design, too.

Curl the tinsel into balls before sewing it on the cushion.

Stick the stripes on with craft glue.

Cushion 5

Sew a piece of tinsel around the edge of the cushion, and then sew more tinsel onto the front and back. Try using ribbons, buttons, or pieces of fun fur.

Cushion 6

Create a dramatic animal pattern, such as these zebra stripes. Simply cut out strips from a piece of felt and glue them straight onto the cushion cover.

Scrap bags

These floppy bag people

are made from scraps of
left-over material and filled
with dried beans.

"Try me I'm
very filling",
yell the lentils.

Play with us,
we're full of beans!

Throw together a scrap bag

Here, catch!

To make a bag

Use the scrap bag pattern to measure the size of your bag. Cut out a piece of fabric and fold it in half.

Fold it in half.

LEAVE A HOLE

STITCHING LINE

Scrap bag pattern

Follow this
pattern to help
you with the size.

FOLD THE FABRIC HERE

STITCHING LINE

LEAVE A HOLE

Leave an opening
at the top.

Back stitch around
the open sides.

Turn the bag
inside out.

Fill it up with
lentil beans.

To finish it off,
stitch up the hole
at the top.

Pin it together

Sew up the sides

Turn inside out and fill up

Close it up

Back stitch

A good stitch to use is back stitch because it completely seals the sides. Don't be fooled into thinking you can do a simple running stitch, if you do the beans will fall out!

See page 56 for back stitch instructions.

Sew or use PVA glue to attach the faces.

Scrap bag games

Target practice

Set up a target area around a bucket and challenge your family to score high. Make up the rules yourself!

Juggling

Start with two then build up your bags. A perfect practice for a rainy day.

Play catch

Throw a bag for a friend to catch. If they miss they go down on one knee, miss again they go down on two knees, and so on until they are lying down.

Bad luck! To score 100 it must go right into the bowl.

100

50

25

Good shot, that's 100 points!

Hello Dolly!

Dolly's awake!

Pack up her nightdress, pop on her clothes,
and she's ready for the day ahead.

Dolly's bag

Make a pretty pouch to keep Dolly in – find out how on page 74.

Dolly's dressed up for the day.

These are Dolly's night-time things.

Goodnight Dolly!

Shhh, Dolly's asleep.

Take out her pillow, put on her nightdress, and Dolly
is ready for bed. And don't forget her teddy!

Dolly's
pillow

Dolly's
nightdress

Dolly's
teddy

Two dollies in one

These two dolls are really
one doll! One side of her
head has an awake face.
Turn her over for her
sleeping face.

Make your own two-sided doll

Snip and sew your own "Hello/ Goodnight Dolly". Use plain cotton fabric and the pattern on page 104.

You will need:

- Dolly pattern
- cotton fabric
- pins
- scissors
- sewing thread
- stuffing
- embroidery thread
- pencil

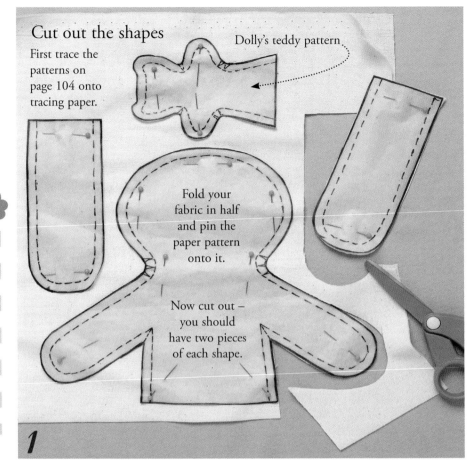

Cut out the shapes

First trace the patterns on page 104 onto tracing paper.

Dolly's teddy pattern

Fold your fabric in half and pin the paper pattern onto it.

Now cut out – you should have two pieces of each shape.

1

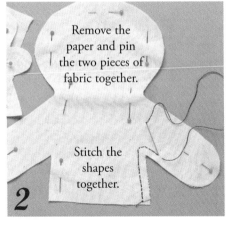

Remove the paper and pin the two pieces of fabric together.

Stitch the shapes together.

2

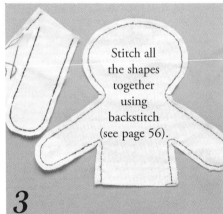

Stitch all the shapes together using backstitch (see page 56).

3

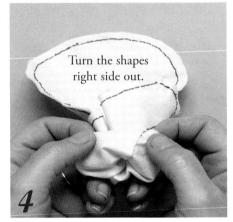

Turn the shapes right side out.

4

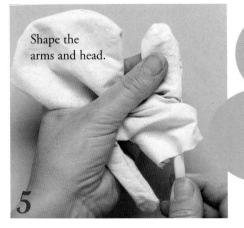

Shape the arms and head.

5

Handy tip

Use a blunt pencil to help shape your doll. Push gently and carefully so you don't break the stitching.

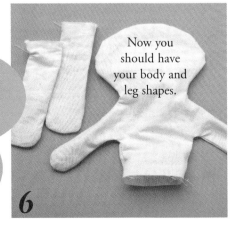

Now you should have your body and leg shapes.

6

Push in the stuffing, a little at a time.

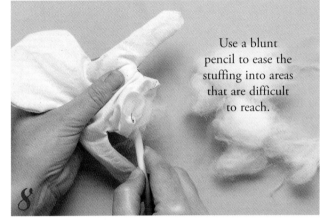

Use a blunt pencil to ease the stuffing into areas that are difficult to reach.

8

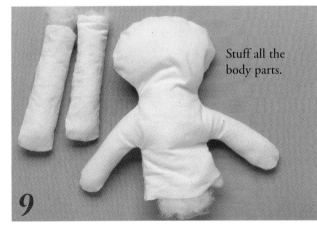

Stuff all the body parts.

9

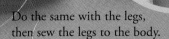

Turn in the edges at the base of the body and stitch it up.

Do the same with the legs, then sew the legs to the body.

10

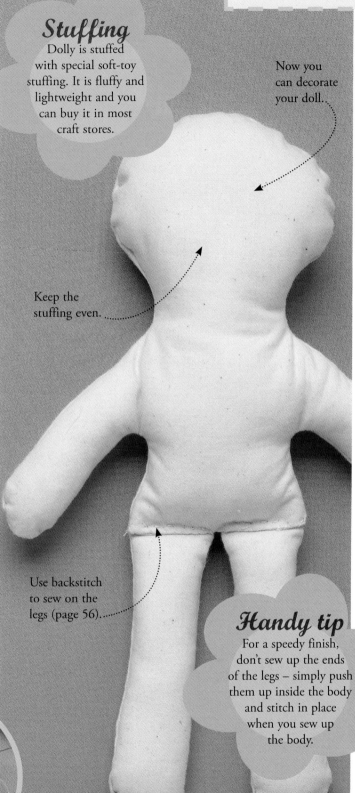

Stuffing

Dolly is stuffed with special soft-toy stuffing. It is fluffy and lightweight and you can buy it in most craft stores.

Now you can decorate your doll.

Keep the stuffing even.

Use backstitch to sew on the legs (page 56).

Handy tip

For a speedy finish, don't sew up the ends of the legs – simply push them up inside the body and stitch in place when you sew up the body.

Sew Dolly's faces

Now you need to make Dolly's awake and sleeping faces. Sew on the features using embroidery stitches, or try fabric pens or felt fabric for easier decoration.

You will need:
- embroidery thread
- needle
- felt pieces
- scissors
- fabric glue
- fabric pens

Sewing faces

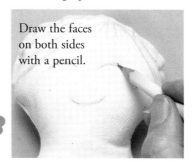

Draw the faces on both sides with a pencil.

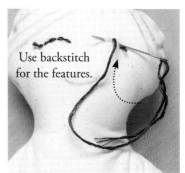

Use backstitch for the features.

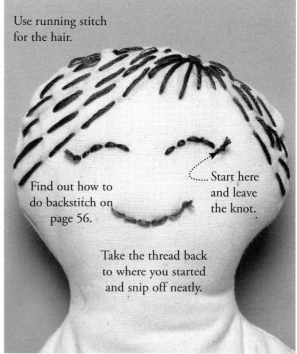

Use running stitch for the hair.

Find out how to do backstitch on page 56.

Start here and leave the knot.

Take the thread back to where you started and snip off neatly.

Fabric-pen faces

Fabric pens are the easiest way to put on Dolly's face.

Don't forget the eyelashes!

Felt faces

You can use felt for faces too! Glue it on using fabric glue.

Cut features out of felt.

Try a cat face

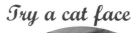

Instead of a doll, why not try making a teddy, a dog, or a cat.

Use stitches, pen, or felt pieces to decorate your cat.

Make Dolly's clothes

Now it's time to design Dolly's clothes. Pick the fabric you like and fashion together some day and night clothes.

You will need:
- pieces of fabric
- sewing thread and needle
- ribbon
- safety pins

Dolly's blouse

Dolly's skirt

Blouse

Cut out a piece of fabric 19 cm x 10 cm (7 1/2 in x 4 in).

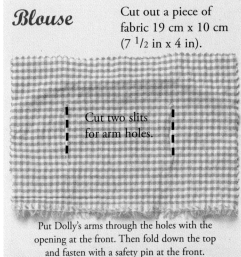

Cut two slits for arm holes.

Put Dolly's arms through the holes with the opening at the front. Then fold down the top and fasten with a safety pin at the front.

Skirt and nightie

Cut a piece of fabric 38 cm x 15 cm (14 in x 6 in).

Fold over the top and the bottom and pin in place.

Sew down the folds using running stitch (see page 56).

...Sew the stitch close to the bottom of the fold.

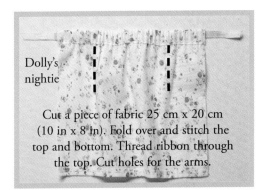

Dolly's nightie

Cut a piece of fabric 25 cm x 20 cm (10 in x 8 in). Fold over and stitch the top and bottom. Thread ribbon through the top. Cut holes for the arms.

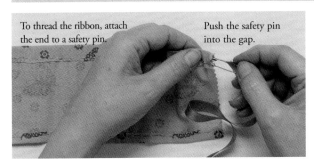

To thread the ribbon, attach the end to a safety pin.

Push the safety pin into the gap.

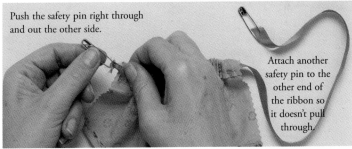

Push the safety pin right through and out the other side.

Attach another safety pin to the other end of the ribbon so it doesn't pull through.

Push the fabric along the ribbon to gather it up.

Remove the safety pins.

Wrap the skirt around Dolly and tie the ribbons in a bow at the back.

Dolly pattern

Here is the pattern for the doll on page 98.
It's shown here actual size, so simply trace the patterns and cut out the material to match.

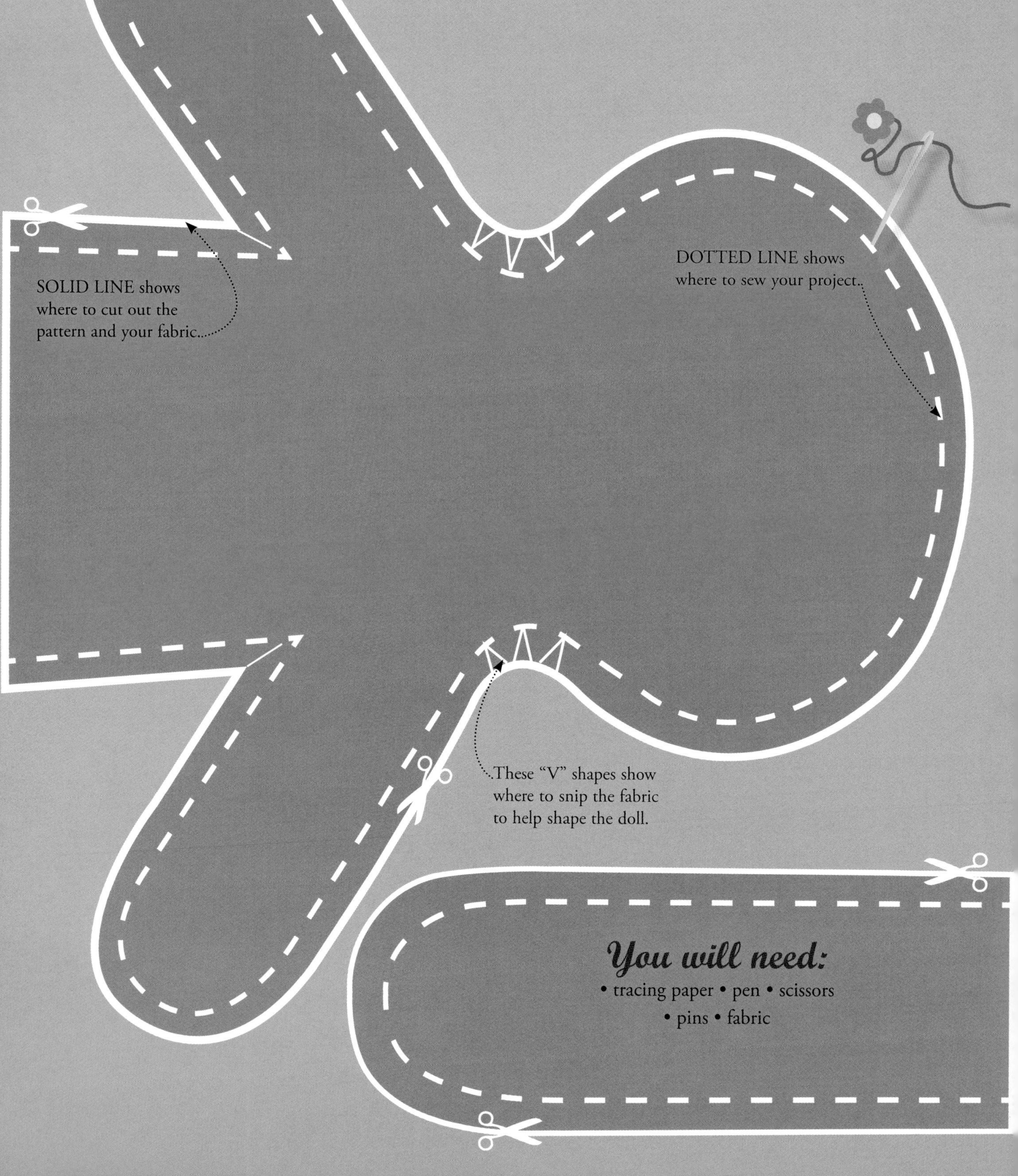

DOTTED LINE shows where to sew your project.

SOLID LINE shows where to cut out the pattern and your fabric.

These "V" shapes show where to snip the fabric to help shape the doll.

You will need:
• tracing paper • pen • scissors
• pins • fabric

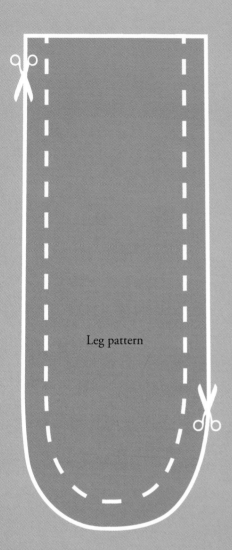

Leg pattern

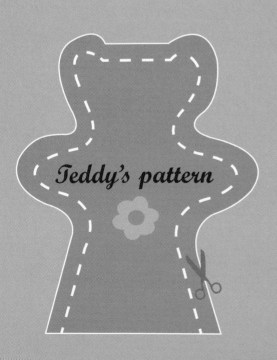

Teddy's pattern

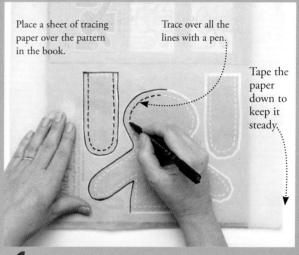

Place a sheet of tracing paper over the pattern in the book.

Trace over all the lines with a pen.

Tape the paper down to keep it steady.

1 Trace the shapes

Carefully cut around the lines.

2 Cut them out

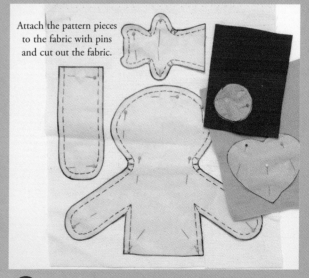

Attach the pattern pieces to the fabric with pins and cut out the fabric.

3 Pin them to the fabric

Lavender bags

Dried lavender flowers

Dried lavender

Lavender smells beautiful. The dried flowers give off a strong scent – they're perfect for stuffing these little pyramid bags.

You will need:
• cotton fabric
• needle, pins, and thread
• dried lavender flowers
• dried rice

Put the right sides together.

1 Cut out fabric

Cut two squares of thin fabric 10 cm x 10 cm (4 in x 4 in).

Sew around three edges using backstitch (see page 56).

Fill the bag with two tablespoons of dried rice and one tablespoon of dried lavender flowers.

Turn the bag right side out.

Don't stuff it too full.

2 Turn the right sides out

3 Fill up the bag

If you cut your fabric squares smaller, you can make mini pyramids too.

To finish, bring the sides of the bag together to make a triangle shape.

Turn in the edges and neatly stitch them together.

Sew on pretty ribbon or trimming and stitch into place.

Handy tip
Use fabric glue to hold the decorations in place.

4 Stitch together

5 Finishing touch

Sweet smells

If you can't find dried lavender, potpourri makes a good alternative – scents like roses or pine work well.

You could try

Personalize your bag by using the embroidery stitches you've learned from the embroidery section. Sew your design to the front before you sew the squares together at step 1.

Patchwork patterns

Mix and match your fabrics- Try this simple patchwork design and create a comfy quilt for your toys.

You will need:
- Nine 55 sq mm squares of cotton fabric
- sewing thread • needles and pins
- Nine 45 sq mm paper templates

Place a square of paper in the middle of the fabric.

1 Cut out the fabric

Fold the fabric over the edge of the paper.

Loosely sew the fabric to the paper.

2 Sew to the paper...

Sew all the way round using big stitches.

3 ...all the way round

Over-sew the edge, but try not to sew through the paper..

Then remove the loose stitches.

4 Join up the squares

Remove the paper templates after the squares have been sewn up.

Because the stitches are large and loose they will be easy to unpick.

Sewing tip

When joining the squares, hold two together firmly and over-stitch the join using small stitches. Make sure you just catch the edge of the fabric – not the paper.

5 Finishing off

Cut a piece of felt the same size as the patchwork and pin it in place. Finish off by sewing them together with a running stitch.

Project ideas

- **Quilt** - Design a comfy quilt for your toys like this one.
- **Cushions** - Make colourful cushions of all shapes and sizes.
- **Bag** - Design a handy bag for your sewing kit.

Z Z Z Z

Ribbons

Ribbons and braids make great finishing touches to your projects. Try a strip of ric-rac as shown here.

Packing Presents

It's the night before Christmas and as dusk falls stockings are waiting to be filled through the night. So surprise Santa with these bright ones!

Attach a tag to the top so that you can hang it up.

Stick all of the decorations on with a fabric glue. It will say on the tube if it is suitable.

Cut out two sock shapes and stick them together with a fabric glue.

Make them big, Santa's stuffing more in this year!

Cut Rudolph's face shape out of felt and stick it to the stocking. Use different colours for the features.

A Stitch in Time

To jazz up the stocking, try your hand at blanket stitch (see page 115) around the edges.

Start the stitch by putting the needle through about 1 cm (¹/2 in) away from the edge.

Bring the thread under the needle as you pull it down and through – it's as simple as that!

Fill me up to the brim

Stick 'em Up!

If the stockings are ready then it's almost Christmas Day. Hurray! Hang it up and wait for Santa, or you could make one as a gift for someone special.

These felt snowflakes prove that you don't have to use a lot of colours to get a great Christmas look.

The best thing about these stockings is that you can use them year after year.

Winter woollies

Soft and squashy felt decorations
hang around with fuzzy pompoms.

How to stitch some woollies

Collect together colourful felts and threads.

Cut out two shapes, sew them up using blanket stitch, stuff them with something soft, and decorate with sparkly sequins. Turn to page 39 to make pompoms.

NEEDLE THREADER

GOLD OR SILVER THREAD

LOTS OF DIFFERENT COLOURED FELT

SEQUINS AND RIBBONS FOR DECORATION

Needles and pins

You will need:
- embroidery needles – use a needle threader to help you thread a needle
- Glue
- Stuffing

PINS

COLOURED THREAD

PVA GLUE

SCISSORS

SOFT TOY STUFFING

Cutting shapes

Turn to page 142 to find templates.

Cover the page with a piece of tracing paper.

Trace over the shapes with a pencil.

Glue a heart to the triangle shape.

Angels and fairies

Cut out, stitch, and stuff

Pin your template onto a piece of folded felt and cut it out.

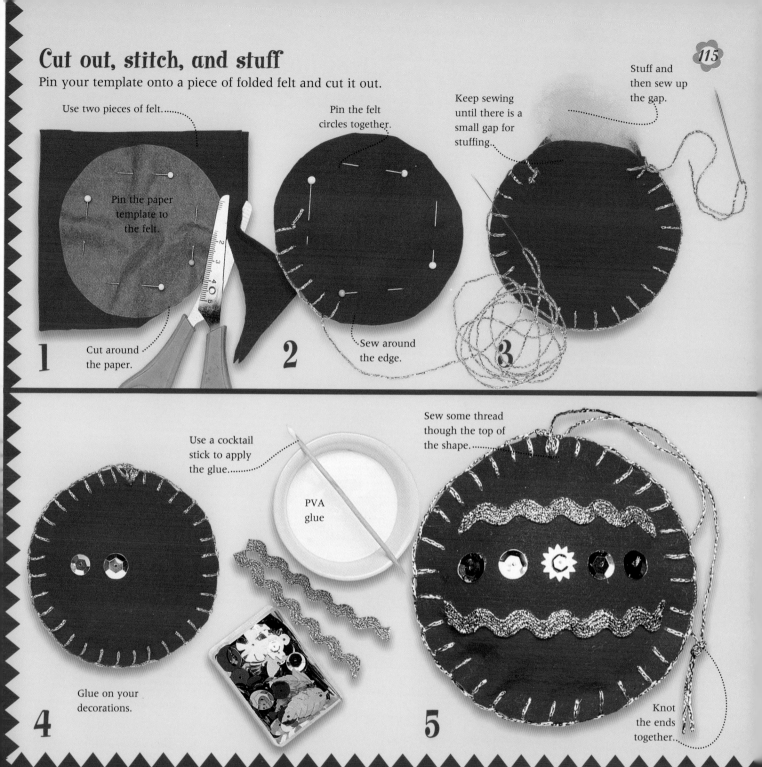

Use two pieces of felt.....

Pin the felt circles together.

Keep sewing until there is a small gap for stuffing.

Stuff and then sew up the gap.

Pin the paper template to the felt.

Cut around the paper.

Sew around the edge.

Use a cocktail stick to apply the glue.....

PVA glue

Sew some thread though the top of the shape.....

Glue on your decorations.

Knot the ends together.

Blanket stitch This stitch looks great and is easy to do, but keep it neat!

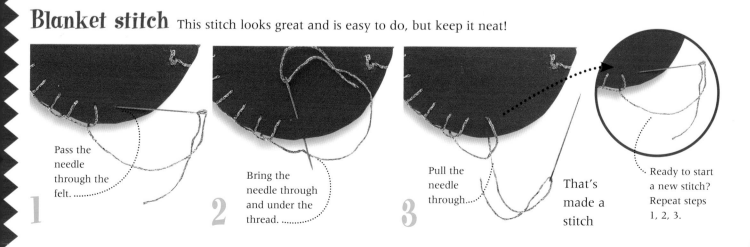

Pass the needle through the felt.

Bring the needle through and under the thread.

Pull the needle through.

That's made a stitch

Ready to start a new stitch? Repeat steps 1, 2, 3.

Button badges

Make you own badges -

Buttons do more than fasten your coat. Jazz them up and they make great badges, too! These button bases are a good place to start.

Cut out a circle of card a little bigger than the button top.

Draw around the edge of the circle before cutting out.

Place the button top in the centre of the fabric.

Push the fabric onto the metal hooks.

1 Make a template

2 Cut out the fabric

3 Fix the fabric on

Keep going until all the fabric is fixed tight.

Slip a safety pin through the loop at the back.

Press the back on until it snaps shut.

4 Snap on the back

Buttons

Button bases that you cover yourself can be found in craft shops and are handy when you want buttons to match your clothes. Larger sizes make great badges.

Wobbly eyes are always fun.

A gingerbread man made of felt.

All-sorts

Don't throw your old clothes away! Reuse your favourite fabrics to make some fun buttons. Find pieces that are already embroidered or decorated with beads and sequins, or add your own decoration by sewing or glueing on felt shapes and wobbly eyes.

Stretchy T-shirts work well, too.

Pick out a design feature, such as a flower.

Use lace trimmings for decoration.

Look out for fabric with pretty sewn motifs for an instant effect.

Cup cakes

They look good enough to eat! These little cakes can be delicious pin cushions, tasty brooches, or look simply scrumptious on a plate.

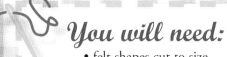

You will need:
- felt shapes cut to size (use the patterns at the front of the book)
- skeins of embroidery silk
- embroidery needle
- stuffing

Decoration

Back shape

Front shape

Front only......

Use lots of little short stitches.

Place the front and back together...

Sew the front and back together.

1 Cut out some pastry

2 Sew on the jam

3 Stitch together

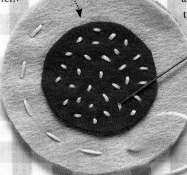

Fill it with stuffing – but not too much.

......Leaving a small gap, pull the thread to gather up the fabric.

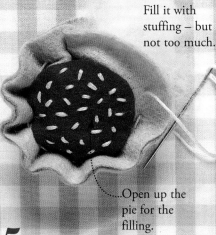

......Open up the pie for the filling.

Sew up the gap and fasten off.

4 Gather it up

5 Stuff the jam tart

6 Stitch it up

Cup cakes

Cherry bakewell
Cut a red felt circle for the cherry.

Chocolate cake
Cut a swirl of pink felt for icing.

Jam tart
Yellow stitches look like little seeds.

Sugar-strand cake
Colourful stitches look like sugar strands.

Brooches

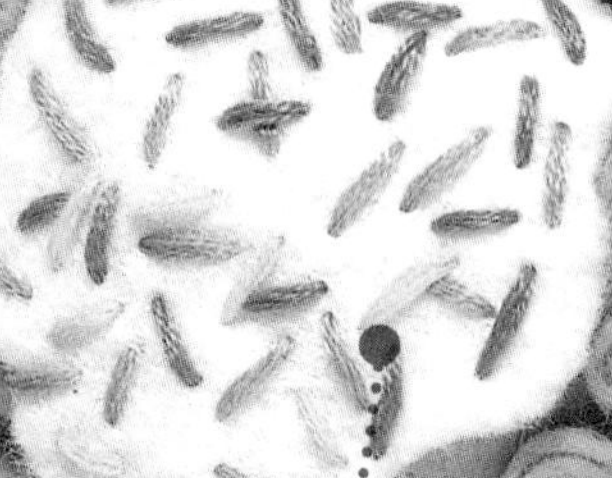

Sew a safety pin to the back.

Pin cushion

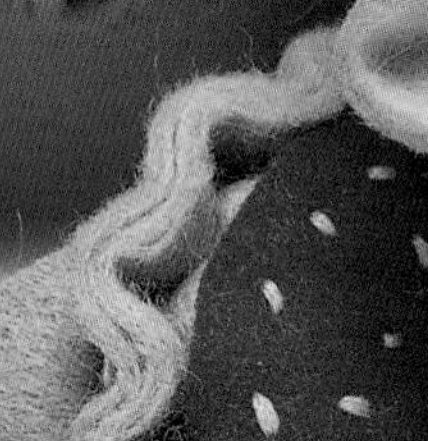

Gift ideas
• **Brooch** - Sew a safety pin to a mini cup cake.
• **Pin cushion** - Pop in your sewing kit as a pin cushion.
• **Birthday cake** - Give one to a friend to celebrate a special occasion!

Fold-away game mats

Anywhere and everywhere – unwrap your mat and you're set up to play a game.

Your mat will need to fold up small enough to fit in your box.

Sticky felt tray

Felt is a good material to use because felt sticks to felt, so the pieces will stay on your board – even when Dad turns a sharp corner!

Cut out a piece of white felt, 30 cm by 30 cm (12 in by 12 in).

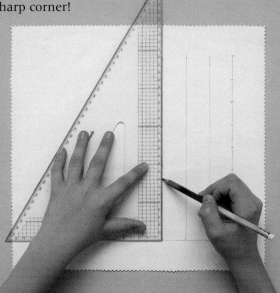

With a ruler mark out every 2.5 cm (1 in) across and down.

Draw in the lines making sure you have 10 boxes by 10 boxes in the centre of the felt.

Colour in every other square. No coloured square should be next to another coloured square.

Snakes and ladders

Your board can be adapted to snakes and ladders, draughts, chess, or any other board game. Just cut out felt shapes to suit your game.

Ready to play

Just unfold and you're ready to play.

Cover up!

wear your art on your clothes,
and keep the sun off too!

Graffi T-shirt
make your mark

Fabric pens are the easiest way to decorate a
T-shirt. Draw your design straight on, then
iron it to make it permanent.

Remember to put
paper or card inside
the T-shirt to stop th
ink going through.

you will need:
• White or light-coloured cotton T-shirt
• Fabric pens

I'm looking at you!

T-shirts

White and pale-coloured T-shirts work best when decorating or dying. If you use a dark T-shirt the decoration won't show as clearly. So get out your old T-shirts and cover up!

Hey! Look at me I look good like that.

Pack up all your stuff in me!

Transform your clothes

Crazy faces

You could use any material to decorate your hats and bags, but felt is a great one to use. It is easy to cut and can be stuck onto other material easily using PVA or fabric glue.

Cut out the shapes.

Practise your face shapes on newspaper first. Then cut them out.

Use the paper templates to draw on to the fabric.

what to do
• Practise your shapes on a piece of newspaper.
• Use your newspaper template to cut out the felt shapes.
• Glue them into position.

Glue the shapes.

PVA glue

Stick into position.

You will need:
• Scraps of fabric, such as felt
• Newspaper
• Scissors
• PVA or fabric glue

Tie-dye T-shirts

The secret of tie-dye is the elastic bands. By tying them tightly the dye will not colour the tied bits, leaving swirls of pattern. When you are dying fabrics, make sure you read and follow the instructions on the dye packet.

Tie the bands

Scrunch up pieces of your T-shirt and tie elastic bands tightly to each little scrunch.

⭐ **Ask an adult** to help with hot water.

Follow the guidelines on the packet.

Mix up the dye

Now dunk your T-shirt into the dye and leave for however long the instructions tell you. Use rubber gloves.

Dunk in a T-shirt

Take it out and rinse it

Remove the bands

Rinse the T-shirt until the colour stops running out. Remove the elastic bands to reveal the twisty, swirly pattern. Then hang it up in the sun to dry.

Remember to use a light T-shirt otherwise the dye won't show.

The more elastic bands you use, the more patterns you get.

Make me some clothes somebody!

Fabric – it's what the clothes we wear are made of! It can be soft, furry, scratchy, strong, or stretchy. Yarns can be woven or knitted to make all kinds of garments.

Fabric

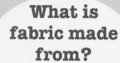

Imagine our world without fabric – we would probably catch a cold without clothes. Furniture is covered in fabric so it's soft and comfortable to sit on.

What is fabric made from?

WOOL comes from sheep, SILK from silk worms, COTTON from cotton plants, LINEN from flax plants. These are all natural products.

When was fabric invented?

The Egyptians first wove cotton into cloth about 14,000 years ago. The Romans built the first wool factory 1,500 years ago.

How is fabric made?

Fabric is usually woven from yarns like wool and cotton. Wool is sheared off the sheep (like a hair cut), then spun into woollen yarn. Yarn can be woven into fabric – see page 128 to try weaving for yourself.

Lycra, nylon, and polyester

Fabrics like these are called synthetic because they are man-made in laboratories. They are more like plastics than fabric.

How your fabric can help others

Take the clothes you've grown out of to charity shops. They will not only be used by someone else but they will make money for charity too.

Look out for labels

Many clothes and other fabrics can be reused or recycled. Look at the labels – this one tells you the fabric is wool.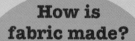

Recycling fabric

Remake clothes and fabric into something else. See the projects in this section for some good ideas. If the fabric is falling apart, it can be made into filling for mattresses and insulation. So recycle your old towels, bed sheets, table linen, and curtains.

Rag mats

Revive old rags

Collect up material and old clothes, cut them into strips, and weave them into pretty mats.

To make strips longer, knot them together.

Cut long strips of cloth 2 cm (1 in) wide.

Cutting the strips

Cut the material into long strips. Use one colour for the main weave that goes up and down, called the "warp", and lots of colours and fabrics for the "weft" – the material the goes across.

Use any old fabric.

How to start

Use a cardboard sheet for your weaving frame. Cut an even number of slits at the top and bottom. Knot together lots of the same colour strips to make one very long strip.

12 slits ......

...... Cut the slits 1 cm (½ in) apart.

Cardboard sheet 20 x 30 cm (8 x 12 in)

12 slits ......

Slip the fabric into the first slit.

Thread the fabric through each slit in turn, around and around from front to back.

Weaving the weft

Weave the strips over and under the main colour – the warp. Pull the strip all the way through before starting the next line. Leave a bit at the beginning and weave it back on itself to anchor it.

When you reach the end, turn the strip around and go back again. ......

Weave in the other direction, tucking under where you went over.

Knot a new fabric strip onto the end and carry on weaving.

Continue weaving – don't do it too tight.

Weave the last colour and secure the end by weaving it back on itself. ......

Finishing off

Turn the board over.

Cut through the fabric strips.

Knot pairs of strips together. ......

Gently pull the fabric strips through the slits.

...... Trim them to the same length.

Making friends

They're woolly, they're soft, they're your bobble-hat and glove friends! Have you grown out of your woolly warmers? Then transform them into cuddly creatures.

KNOW YOUR STUFF
Jumpers and other items made of wool can be respun – the fibres are used again, to make new clothes.

How to make woolly friends

Take a glove and decide what shape you want it to be. Turn to page 56 to find out how to do back stitch, which will help you when you sew up the fingers.

1.

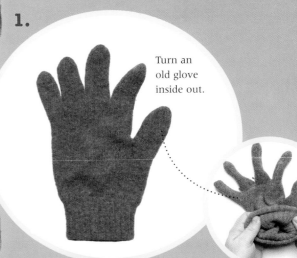

Turn an old glove inside out.

Make new friends from old

All kinds of gloves can be used – from baby mittens to Dad's big gloves. Experiment with how many fingers to use.

> Try stuffing your old hats to make us!

I'm a glove with short fingers...

I've got a thumb nose...

......Use all the fingers to make my hair.

2.

Sew up the middle two fingers and the thumb...

Turn the glove right side out again.

Push out the fingers that haven't been sewn up.

Cotton wool and old tights are great for stuffing gloves......

3.

Now make a face using stitches, fabric scraps, or buttons.

Stuff the glove.

Sew up the bottom.

Hold onto your hats!
Don't chuck them, recycle them.
Ask your family to give you their old hats.
The more you have, the more bobble-hat
people you can make.

This bow came from a hat........

Put a bow on your hat and make me – Betty Bow

KNOW YOUR STUFF
Over 70% of the world's population uses second-hand clothes.

What to use for stuffing
You can use almost any soft fabric for
stuffing. Old socks and tights are
probably the pieces of clothing people
throw away most often, so gather
them up before they go!

A quick sewing lesson

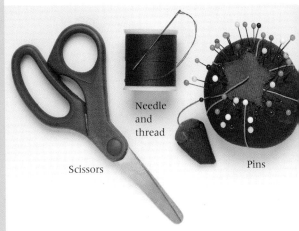

Scissors

Needle and thread

Pins

Back stitch
Back stitch is a good stitch to use because it
keeps the stuffing in well. Practise on a piece
of material before you start.

Knot the end of the thread and push the needle down and up through the fabric.

Pull the needle all the way through to the knot.

Now push the needle half way between the knot and the dangling thread.

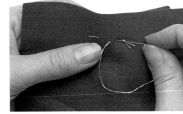

Bring the needle up in front of the dangling cotton.

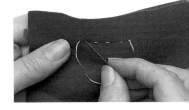

Repeat these steps and sew over the last stitch to finish off.

How to make Bob Bobble

Try to find two hats that are about the same size. Ideally, Bob should have one hat without a bobble, and one hat with a bobble. But you can always make your own pom-pom to go on top.

Find two hats, about the same size.

Sew on buttons or fabric scraps to make Bob Bobble's face.

Old buttons

6. Now make the face

1. Pin the hats together

Turn the top hat upside down.

Turn the bottom hat inside out.

Place the top hat into the bottom hat.

Pin the edges together.

Sew up the opening neatly.

5. Sew up the gap

2. Sew the hats together

Sew along the pins, leaving a 12 cm (5 in) opening at the end.

Turn the hats right-side-out through the opening.

Keep stuffing until Bob feels really full.

4. Stuff

Push your stuffing through the opening.

3. Turn right-side-out

Pocket purses

Don't chuck your old clothes – they might provide perfect pocket purses!

I'm just right for your pocket money!

✂

How to make a purse

Search out an old piece of clothing with a pocket on the outside – one with a zip or button is ideal. Cut around the pocket with pinking shears (scissors with zig-zag edges) and you have your pocket purse – it's as easy as that!

Pinking shears prevent the edges from fraying.

Pinking shears

Trouser bags

Rescue your favourite old jeans and turn them into these cool bags.

Recycle your trousers and skirts,

make glam bags for school,

and purses to pop in the pockets.

KNOW YOUR STUFF
Even when fabric is so worn out it's falling to bits, it's still worth recycling. It can be used for insulation and filling for mattresses.

Fabric

How to make a glam bag

Recycle old trousers

to make these glamorous bags. Simply cut off the legs, sew up the opening, and attach a handle.

Needle, cotton and pins

1.

Cut off the trouser tops just above the legs......

2.

Turn inside out.

......Turn the top inside out and pin the two bottom edges together.

......Stitch.

3. Turn right way out.

Use pinking shears so the material won't fray.

Pin the strap in place.....

Sew it tightly.

Add a strap

Use the material from one leg to make your strap. Cut a length about 3 cm (1 in) wide and sew it in place.

Glam it up

When you have finished your bag, decorate it with beads, badges, and bows. Then there are all those handy pockets to fill!

Make a matching pocket purse......

Fancy strap

You could use a ribbon for the strap, like this pink velvet one.

Comfy cushions

Snuggle up to your favourite T-shirt or jeans after you have grown out of them. Brighten up your bedroom with these quirky cushions.

Clothing cushions
As well as reusing your T-shirts, try making Glam bags (page 136–7) into cushions too.

.... The pockets are still handy.

These look cosy – now you can enjoy your favourite clothes for longer!

Make a T-shirt cushion

Take a clean T-shirt

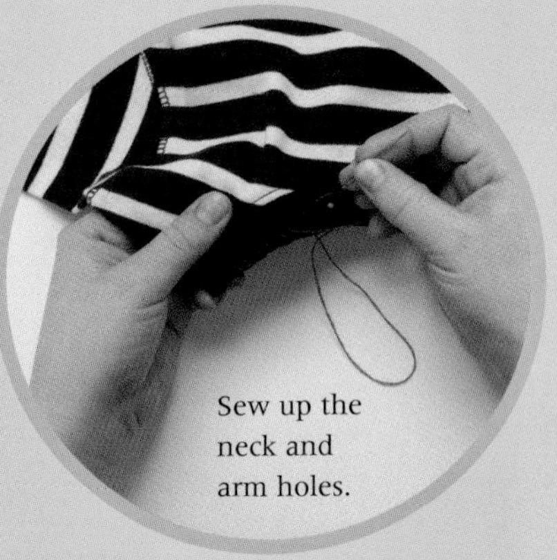

Sew up the neck and arm holes.

Sew it up

Use more old clothes for the stuffing.

Stuff it

Cut shapes from other material and sew them on as decoration.

Sew up the bottom of the shirt.

Sew it up and decorate it

KNOW YOUR STUFF

Most discarded clothes are still in good condition. DON'T BURY THEM IN A LANDFILL – give them to charity instead.

Crafty kit · Here's a guide to the materials

Fabric pens

FABRIC PENS • You can create some very effective designs using fabric pens (for example, when decorating Pirate Pete). Always put some paper or card beneath the fabric you are colouring to stop the ink running through, and take care not to get ink on your clothes. Follow the instructions on the packet to ensure the best results.

Bits and bobs

To finish off your projects nicely, you will often need bits and bobs. To finish off projects, you will often need odd household items, so keep your eyes open for things you can use in your arty crafts, such as:
- buttons and beads
- ribbon
- old paper
- anything with a texture that would work well for printing, like empty cotton reels, used-up pens, and old sponges.

★ **Ask an adult.** You will se this sign if you need to as an adult to help you.

Scissors

used to make the projects in this book.

Pins and needles

WOOL • For knitting, woolly webs, and cross-stitch, you will need wool, which you buy in balls.

DARNING NEEDLE • If you are sewing with wool, you will need a darning needle, which has a big hole, or "eye".

KNITTING NEEDLES • Come in different sizes. In this book they are 4 mm (no. 8).

SEWING NEEDLE • For sewing with thin thread, you will need a sewing needle with a small eye – not a darning needle. If you have trouble threading a needle, you can buy a simple, cheap tool to make it easier.

PINS • Always pin material before you sew it.

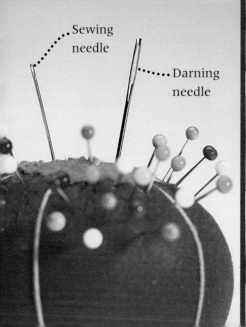

Sewing needle

Darning needle

Backstitch

This quick, strong stitch is a bit like a doubled-up running stitch. When you use it to sew Pirate Pete, it will stop his filling from falling out.

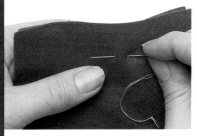

Knot the end of the thread. Push the needle down and up through the fabric.

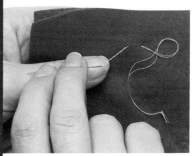

Pull the needle all the way through to the knot.

Put the needle between the knot and the dangling thread.

Bring the needle up ahead of the dangling thread.

Repeat these steps and sew over a few stitches to finish off.

Fabrics

EMBROIDERY FABRIC • In order to make the cross-stitch patterns, you will have to buy special fabric called BINKA. It has big holes that you can easily put wool through.

COTTON FABRIC • For Pirate Pete and friends, white cotton is the best material. Old sheets and pillowcases would be perfect.

Beads for noses

Buttons for eyes

Index

Aida fabric 54, 55, 66
Alien 29
Angels 112, 113, 114
Animals 28, 29, 78, 79, 93

Backstitch 56, 80, 97, 130, 132, 141
Badges 116, 117, 137
Bag 16, 26, 27 57, 72, 73, 74, 75, 86, 87, 88, 89, 94-7, 98, 109, 124, 135, 137, 138
Bangle 86
Beads 34, 140, 141
Bean bags 76-81, 94-7
Beanie hat 34
Belt 14
Big knitting 38-9
Binka fabric 64, 141
Birthday cake 119
Bits and bobs 140
Blanket 24
Blanket stitch 56, 60, 57, 61, 82, 84, 110, 114, 115
Bobble hat 31, 34, 35, 130, 131, 132, 133
Bows 90, 91, 93, 132, 137
Bracelet 10, 12, 14, 16
Braids 17, 109
Brooch 60, 69, 85, 118, 119
Bubble wrap 90, 92
Button badges 116-17
Button bases 116
Buttons 34, 57, 93, 116, 117, 133, 134, 140, 141

Calico 55
Cacti 90, 91
Casting on 13, 14, 19
Casting off 13, 20-21
Cat 29, 77, 79, 102
Chain stitch 61, 56
Charity shops 127, 139
Christmas 110, 111, 112-15
Christmas tree 85, 112-13

Clothes 117, 122-5, 126, 127, 130, 132, 134, 135, 136, 139
Cotton 10, 72, 127, 141
Cover up! 122-23
Cow 79
Crafts 140
Crafty kit 140-41
Cross-stitch 54, 56, 59, 60, 61, 62-67
Cup cake 61, 118-19
Cushion 54, 55, 90-95, 109, 138-9

Darning needle 32, 64, 141
Decorations 110, 111, 112-15, 117, 137
Dolly 36, 37, 98-105
Double-knit wool 10
Dye 93, 122, 125

Egg box 53
Embroidery 50-69, 117
Embroidery needle 10
Egyptians 127
Equipment 140-41

Fabric 72, 126-7, 141
Fabric pens 81, 122, 140
Faces 124, 130, 131
Fairies 112, 113, 114
Felt 72, 73, 93, 108, 110, 111, 112, 113, 114, 115, 117, 120, 121
Felt flowers 86-87
Finger knitting 24-5
Finger puppet 24-5
Finishing off 14
Flower 36, 56, 86-7, 117
Fold-away game mats 120-21
Frame 55, 58, 66, 129
Friends 30-31, 130-34
Fun with wool 40-49
Fur 93

Game mats 120, 121
Games 97, 120, 121
Garter stitch 11, 19
Get weaving 46-47
Ghost 77, 78

Gingerbread man 117
Girl 78, 79
Glam bags 135, 136-7, 138
Gloves 130, 131
Glue 93, 97, 110, 114, 115, 124

Hair clip 74, 86
Handy knits 14-15
Hanging softies 84-5
Hat 10, 31, 34, 35, 36-7, 124, 130, 132, 133

Jam jar 53
Jewellery 72, 85
Juggling 97

Key 82, 83
Key ring 69, 85
Knit stitch 11
Knitted cords 11
Knitted pals 30-31
Knitted purses 26-7
Knitting 8-39
Knitting doll 10, 12-13
Knitting needle 10, 141
Krazy knits 28-9

Lace 72, 117
Lazy daisy stitch 56, 59
Letters 64, 65
Linen 127
Looms 48, 49
Lycra 127

Necklace 85
Needles 10, 72, 141
Needle threader 21, 72, 114
Nylon 10, 127

Owl 28, 29

Packing presents 110-11
Paint 93
Paper 140
Patchwork 108-9
Patterns 77, 90, 91, 93, 96-7, 108-9, 125, 142
Pens 81, 121, 122

Picture 58, 63, 66, 67
Pin cushion 53, 55, 73, 109, 118, 119
Pinking shears 73, 134
Pins 72, 141
Pirate Pete 76-81, 140, 141
Pixel pix 68-9
Plain stitch 24
Plait 78, 79
Pocket locket 61, 82-3
Pocket purses 134-35, 137
Polyester 127
Pom-pom 36, 37, 39, 114, 133
Pouch 72, 74-5, 98
Presents 110, 111
Project ideas 109
Puppet 24-5
Purse 10, 26-7, 134, 135, 137

Quilt 109

Rag mats 128-9
Reindeer 110, 111
Ribbon 49, 72, 93, 109, 114, 115, 137, 140
Ribbon bag 88-9
Ric-rac 109
Romans 127
Rudolph 110, 111
Running stitch 56, 108

Sampler 67
Santa 110, 111
Scarf 10, 31, 34, 35, 37, 39
Scrap bags 94-5
Sequins 114, 115, 117
Sewing 32, 33, 70-139
Silk 127
Slip-knot 19
Snakes and ladders 121
Snowflakes 111
Snowman 77, 78
Soft toys 30, 31, 76-81, 108-9
Stitch directory 56
Stitches 11, 50-69
Stockings 111, 112-15

Stocking stitch 11
Stripes 90, 91. 93
Stuffing 28, 76, 81, 84,
      94-7, 101, 114, 115,
      118, 131, 132, 133,
      139
Tapestry 54, 68
Teddy 30, 31, 32-3, 34-5,
      99, 105
Templates 77, 80, 81,
      96-7, 108-9, 110, 111,
      114, 115, 124, 142
Thread 11, 72, 141
Tie-dye 125
Tinsel 90, 93
Toys 30, 31, 76-81,
      108-9 *see also* Teddy
Trimmings 72
Trouser bags 135, 136-7
T-shirt 54, 57, 60-61,
      117, 122-23, 138, 139

Warp 128, 129
Weaving 44-9, 128, 129
Weft 128, 129
Winter woollies 112-15
Wobbly eyes 117
Wool 10, 11, 42, 43, 46,
      47, 78, 79, 112-15,
      127, 130-31, 141
Woolly webs 42-5, 46, 47
Workbox 52-3

Yarn 10, 11, 126, 127

Zebra stripes 93
Zip 134

Acknowledgements

With thanks to...

Maisie Armah, Eleanor Bates, Charlotte Bull, Billy Bull, James Bull, Luke Bower, Daniel Ceccarelli, Lulu Coulter, Cara Crosby-Irons, Lucas Dyson-Diaz, Seriye Ezigwe, Georgia Grossman, Harry Holmstoel, Sophie Hind, Guy Lowrie, Imogen Lowrie, Max Lowrie, Tilly Lumsden, Sorcha Lyons, Nara Mackenzie, Hanna Moore, Kayla Morgan, Eloise Rakic-Platt, Riley Scott, Louis Stride, Anna Turgoose and Kailen Wilcox.

Penny Smith and Lauren Rosier for editorial and design help.
Dave King for additional photography.

Picture Credits

The publisher would like to thank the following for their kind permission to reproduce their photographs:
(Key: b-bottom; c-centre; f-front; l-left; r-right; t-top; b/g-background)

Corbis Gregor Schuster 135 (B/G); **iStockphoto.com** Tracy Hebden 70-71; Debbie Lund 8-9; Liang Zhang 50-51.

Jacket images *Front* **iStockphoto.com** David Franklin ftr. *Back* **iStockphoto.com** Susan Trigg cb. *Spine* **iStockphoto.com** Susan Trigg t.

All other images © Dorling Kindersley
For further information see: www.dkimages.com